GW00482983

Belfas

Faith in the City

Edited by

Eoin G. Cassidy
Donal McKeown
John Morrow

Irish Centre for Faith and Culture

VERITAS

Published 2001 by
Veritas Publications
7/8 Lower Abbey Street
Dublin 1
Ireland

Email publications@veritas.ie
Website www.veritas.ie

ISBN 1 85390 558 5

A catalogue record for
this book is available
from the British Library.

Veritas books are printed on paper made from the wood pulp of
managed forests. For every tree felled, at least one tree is planted,
thereby renewing natural resources.

Cover design by Colette Dower
Printed in the Republic of Ireland by Betaprint Ltd, Dublin

CONTENTS

Editors

Rev. Dr Eoin G. Cassidy is executive secretary of the Irish Centre for Faith and Culture and a senior lecturer in philosophy at the Mater Dei Institute, a college of Dublin City University. He has published widely in the area of faith and culture and is editor of *Faith and Culture in the Irish Context* (Veritas, 1996) and *Prosperity with a Purpose: What Purpose?* (Veritas, 2000).

Most Rev. Dr Donal McKeown is a modern languages graduate and was ordained priest in 1977. He spent 23 years teaching, most recently as President of St Malachy's College, Belfast. In April 2001, he was ordained as Auxiliary Bishop in his native diocese of Down and Connor.

Rev. Dr John Morrow is a Presbyterian Minister. His doctorate from Queens University, Belfast, explored the role of the Churches in peace and reconciliation in Ireland. He is a founder member of the Corrymeela Community and was its leader for 13 years. In addition to parish work he has worked on the staff of the Irish School of Ecumenics. He has published widely in the area of peace, reconciliation and ecumenism, most notably *Journey of Hope* (Corrymeela Press). He is married with three sons and a daughter.

Preface

IN THE BEGINNING of 1999, a small group of people working in an inner-city community in Belfast were brought together to reflect on the urban cultural reality as they experienced it today, its implications for the churches, and some of the pastoral responses that had emerged in recent years. The project was sponsored by the ICFC (Irish Centre for Faith and Culture).

The project had a modest aim, namely to produce a publication that would make a contribution to the ongoing work of the main Christian denominations in seeking to redress the increasing sense of alienation from the Christian faith felt by an appreciable section of those who live in inner city Belfast. It is a project that has been stimulated both by an awareness of the difficulties facing those concerned with Christian witness in urban societies throughout the western world, and by a desire to confront the particular nature of the challenge facing those concerned with preaching gospel values in inner city Belfast.

The working party was made up of clergy and lay people from both Protestant and Catholic background that are engaged in the work of faith and community development in inner city Belfast. The ecumenical character of the working party simply reflects the diverse nature of inner city Belfast society. However, it may also give expression to the belief that the gospel will only be effectively preached if the religious dimension to the communal strife in Belfast is both recognised and addressed.

Over the course of the two years the members of the working party have endeavored to listen to the stories of people whose lives were most shaped by the changing urban cultural realities. This included those who had lost all contact with the institutional and others who still retained their links. This publication is designed to allow these disparate voices to be heard in a manner that might facilitate attentiveness to the cultural realities confronting the gospel message in Belfast today. An understanding of these cultural realities clearly demands that they be situated in an historical context. Hence the presence in this publication of a short historical sketch of working class Belfast. It also contains stories that bring to light some tentative faith responses to Belfast urban culture that were made known to the members of the working party.

Reflections by a small working party on the complex urban cultural reality that is inner city Belfast – in what way can such an approach assist the work of Christian witness and evangelisation? Clearly, all that can be achieved through such an approach is to alert others and ourselves to the importance of being attentive to that dynamic that is constituted by the relationship between faith and culture. It is also to be hoped that this publication may stimulate an increasing awareness of the importance for evangelisation in Belfast to allow urban stories to be heard and faith responses to be documented.

Rev. Dr John Morrow
Chairperson of the Working Party

Acknowledgements

THIS PUBLICATION arose from a project set up by the Irish Centre for Faith and Culture (based in St Patrick's College, Maynooth) to reflect on the reality of faith and urban culture in inner-city Belfast. It includes contributions from a wide variety of people with differing viewpoints, not all of which would be shared by all members of the working party or the ICFC. It is the policy of the ICFC, however, to promote a dialogue that is as inclusive as possible. The contributions to this publication reflect the rich tapestry that constitutes the ecumenical nature of the dialogue between faith and culture in inner city Belfast.

The ICFC wishes to acknowledge with gratitude the most generous contribution made by Rev. Dr John Morrow who chaired the proceedings of the working party over a period of two years and who has jointly edited this publication. His unfailing courtesy and dedication to the work of the project was in no small way responsible for its successful outcome. The ICFC also wishes to thank The Most Rev. Dr Donal McKeown, Auxiliary Bishop of Down and Connor, for his invaluable contribution to the publication.

We wish to acknowledge also with gratitude the contribution made by all the members of the working party and in particular those who contributed to the publication. The following is a list of those who were at some stage members of the working party: Sr Miriam Brady, Rev. Leslie Carroll, Cathy Curran, Ken Groves, Cathy Higgins, Rev. Norman Jardine, Sr Kathleen Keane, Sr Ethna Kelly, Rev. Richard Kelly OFM, Rev. David Kerr, Rev. Dr Gary Mason, Eddie McDowell, Rev. Bill Moore, Rev. John Murray, Helen Smith. We also wish to acknowledge with gratitude the assistance of the Rev. John Harvey, Iona Community, to the work of the project, and

Shelagh Livingstone and Rev. Patrick McCafferty for their contributions to the publication.

We wish to acknowledge the following centres, which afforded us hospitality during the course of our two years work: Forthsprings Community Centre, Springfield Road; St Patrick's Parish Centre, Donegal Street; St Malachy's College, Antrim Road; the Bridge Community Centre, Ravenhill Road; the Inter-Church Centre, Elmwood Avenue.

Rev. Professor James McEvoy
Director
ICFC

Rev. Dr Eoin G. Cassidy
Executive Secretary
ICFC

Faith and Culture:
Understanding the Nature of the Connection

Eoin G. Cassidy

THE CHURCHES can play the right notes but in the wrong order. They can also play the right notes in a way that is not capable of being heard. They can also play the wrong notes. This study is motivated by the view that faith is always transmitted and received in a particular cultural context and that 'a faith which does not become culture is a faith which has not been fully received, not thoroughly thought through, not fully lived out'.[1] It is not just that the message proposed by the Christian faith must be tuned to the cultural realities of the recipients, even more important is the realisation that the questions to which the Christian faith is a response emerge from a particular set of cultural presuppositions. Those concerned with evangelisation have always recognised this truth, but we are increasingly becoming ever more aware of the pace of change in contemporary culture and, in consequence, of not just the importance but also the difficulty of being a proficient reader of the 'signs of the times'.

Understanding culture
Culture can be described in a variety of ways, but perhaps the best approach for our purposes is to understand it in its broad anthropological meaning – 'as a cluster of assumptions, values and ways of life'.[2] In this context, culture gives concrete expression to a

community's self-understanding. However, whatever definition one accepts, the important thing to recognise is that culture is not a neutral cluster of behaviour patterns or values, but rather it is the lens through which we view the world. It is a hidden set of control mechanisms that shape our sensibility. As Michael Paul Gallagher perceptively remarks, 'culture can be an unrecognised presence, a highly selective screen between us and our world that decides what we pay attention to and what we ignore. It is all the more potent for being largely concealed in its impact'.[3] He further makes the point that:

> Although nothing about culture is necessary or inevitable, when we swim in this ocean or see through this lens or receive the transmission of this force around us, everything seems utterly normal and neutral. Awakening to its non-neutrality is a first step towards a Christian response to culture in practice.[4]

In approaching the question of the most appropriate way of understanding the relation between the gospel and culture or faith and culture, it is important to recognise that there are two very different approaches that can be taken. These can be described respectively as a dialogical approach and a dialectical approach. 'The dialogue model builds on such gospel images as the leaven that penetrates the dough and insists that to be faithful to the incarnation of Christ one has to embrace the human realities of culture rather than judge them from outside. But the dialectic model reminds Christians of the radical ambiguity of all cultures, of their potential to freeze into destructive and alienating forms, and hence the permanent need or prophetic resistance to any uncritical identification of culture with gospel'.[5] Essentially, we need to adopt both a dialogical and a dialectical approach. Although culture provides the scenario of the infrastructure for the communication of the gospel, it is more than a passive frame of reference. Cultures are human constructions, and as such bring a mixture of shadows and light.

Faith and urban culture: some general comments

One of the most noticeable features of Christianity in an urban culture such as Belfast is the contrast between the religious practice of those from relatively affluent backgrounds and those from the socially or economically deprived areas of the city. Why is this the case? An outside observer might plausibly argue that those who are socially or economically deprived would seem to have far more need of God than their relatively independent and self-sufficient, middle-class, urban neighbours.

One can hardly argue that the causes of the sharp decline in religious practice in the socially deprived areas of a city can be blamed exclusively on the influence of materialism, consumerism or even the supposedly secular influence of the media. Whatever the significance of these factors, there is no evidence that these are any more influential in determining societal values in socially deprived areas than in what could be described as middle-class Belfast. Perhaps one could argue that the Churches are perceived to favour the middle class as distinct from those who view themselves as on the margins of society. However, this begs the question as to whether the Churches were any less middle class fifty or seventy-five years ago, a period that witnessed high religious practice across all social categories. It would seem to turn the parable of 'the eye of the needle' on its head.

The reasons for this increasing alienation from the institutional Church, particularly among this segment of inner urban culture, have not yet been properly articulated. It may be that Church authority has waned or that people are no longer ruled by fear of the afterlife or that Church teaching on social and sexual ethics is perceived as outmoded or that the secular aspects of Sunday such as dressing up are served in some other way. It may be simply that people no longer rely on the Sunday sermon for news or opinions or that the symbolism of the liturgy no longer communicates with a secular urban population. Alternatively, it could be the cumulative effect of the recent scandals that have involved church people. Perhaps, at a deeper level it reflects a perceived impotence of Christianity in the face of the ultimate scandal, the suffering that is visited disproportionately upon marginalised communities in the form of alcohol, drugs, HIV and AIDS.

Lacking a sense of belonging

Alienation from the church is a complex issue but certainly has something to do with a sense of belonging or lack of belonging, perhaps tied in with the residue of the legacy of a long history of low self-esteem linked to unacceptable levels of poverty. In a culture that increasingly measures people's worth in terms of their material success the less well off suffer twice. In some cases they suffer material poverty, but they are also open to another type of poverty that is more corrosive, namely that inner poverty that touches on self-esteem. This can express itself as a rejection of all forms of authority. In the minds of some, the Church is still a very powerful focus of authority, as is also the State. It is surely no coincidence that, in the western democracies, the lowest participation rates in the democratic process come from socially deprived urban areas. In this context, religious indifference or apathy should not be taken too easily at face value. There is evidence to suggest that both political and religious indifference in an inner city context can be a mask that hides the alienation or anger of those who do not perceive themselves to be economic or cultural stakeholders in society.

Authority and authoritarianism

Looking a little closer at the issue of authority, it is interesting to observe that, across all social categories and religious denominations, it is the institution of the Church that is perceived to be the principal barrier to religious faith. This is particularly the case in areas of greatest social deprivation. For some from a Catholic background the words 'church', 'authoritarianism' and 'paternalism' are interchangeable. Yet the question could be asked as to whether the Christian churches, and in particular, the Catholic Church are any more authoritarian or male dominated today than they were fifty years ago. One does not have to be very perceptive to recognise that authoritarianism was not invented in the 1970s or 1990s. In fact, it could be argued that the mainstream Christian churches are less authoritarian today than at any other time in recent history. Nevertheless, fifty years ago they were not perceived to be particularly male dominated or authoritarian, or at least no more so than many public institutions of that period. However, times change and culture changes, and today any society or organization that is not perceived to encourage an egalitarian and participative ethos is increasingly regarded as ethically suspect. This is something acutely felt by women, and not just middle-class women. In this context, the alienation of inner city urban women not only from Roman Catholic Church structures should not be underestimated. It is something that can be situated in the context of the larger struggle for equality in the home as much as in the workplace.

Tracing the map of urban culture

Very few engaged in urban ministry can presume to be in possession of the map that traces the complex and ever-changing web that is urban culture. There are, however, some general comments that one can put forward that may help to provide a context within which at least the interaction between this urban culture and Catholicism can be situated.

- In some of the newer urban housing estates there is very little evidence of community. In many cases people perceive themselves as living disconnected lives – lacking any real sense of belonging – accentuated by the fact that in many housing estates single-parent families are more the norm than the exception. The relevance of the institutional Church in this context is often questioned. For many in this environment, priests and religious are perceived as addressing exclusively sacramental and welfare needs.
- For whatever reason, in the inner city there no longer exists the close identity between people and Church that formerly applied, and there is no longer an understanding and acceptance of the link between life and liturgy that previously pertained. In a previous generation in the Catholic communities, the sodalities provided a bridge between ordinary lives and the institutional church. In the Protestant and Evangelical Churches this link was provided by the Orange Order, the Boy's Brigade and the Girl's Friendly. There is a lack of appropriate bridges in our contemporary urban culture. Religious events do not seem to touch the social realities of urban life.

- In many urban communities in the lower socio-economic bracket, the church is not perceived to be in solidarity with those on the margins, particularly those affected by the street drug culture, which is such a destructive feature of contemporary inner city urban life.
- The community development movement has in recent years led to the growth of many and diverse group expressions related to housing, mutual support, family centers, planning, advice, etc., which are no longer Church sponsored. This new autonomy has left many people with the feeling that the Churches are not relevant to social need.

Spirituality in an inner city culture[6]

As a counterbalance to an over-negative evaluation of Christian identity in urban society, it would be foolish to underestimate the depth of spirituality in inner city culture. One of the most interesting aspects of two recent studies of Dublin inner city faith patterns is the sign of the emergence of new forms of spirituality in inner city Dublin culture. Although the extent of this development must not be exaggerated, it would seem to be nonetheless real. It is a spirituality that is linked to the emergence of new forms of solidarity in inner city communities, a solidarity that in many cases is born out of the need to respond to the scourge of drugs, HIV and AIDS, which threatens to destroy the very fabric of their communities. In many cases, a drug culture is a sign of hopelessness and exclusion and the taking of drugs can be a way of attempting to cloak a lack of self-esteem or an individual's sense of never having been part of society. In this context, one can appreciate the importance of their sense of God or Jesus as one who listens and as one who heals.[7]

This new inner city spirituality shows itself in the strong sense of the importance of finding both an experience of one's own inner spirituality and an experience of community. Furthermore, in this culture there is an increasing recognition that it is in these areas that God is to be found. In this segment of urban culture the initial experience of suffering, through the breakdown in both social relationships and community, has generated a struggle for survival that can result in the creation of a new found solidarity. The extraordinary feature of this lived experience is that in some cases this has led to a re-imaging or re-finding of a Christian God, one who is revealed in and through suffering and the struggle for solidarity. It is a very different image of God to the more familiar individualistic pietistic one that often marks 'middle class' Christian life. Religious individualism has been with us since the nineteenth century and has failed to nourish inner city spirituality because it never had the potential to address the core truths of people's needs, i.e. the longing for intimacy, the need for friendship and the desire for community.

The needs to which I have alluded are universal. However, perhaps the inner city experience offers a privileged point of entry to a genuine Christian spirituality that is grounded in the experience of solidarity. Obviously, experiences of pain and suffering should not be romanticised. In many cases, pain and suffering caused by alcohol, drugs, sexual abuse, betrayal and, most painful of all, the loss of one's child through AIDS, may block the possibility of spiritual growth. Furthermore, one should not underestimate the sense of God's absence that may be experienced by those that suffer from drug abuse. In this context, people may feel a deep-seated alienation, not only from religious belief, but also from Church structures that are perceived to fashion a God who bears little relevance to their lives. If, however, the research is accurate, we could be witnessing signs of a small new beginning, a renewal of Christianity that is rooted in an inner city culture of survival. This is not the survival of the fittest but the flourishing of the weakest in and through their experience of vulnerability. This experience may often be stark and demanding but it would seem to have the potential to evoke an urban spirituality that is rooted in solidarity.

Notes

1   An extract from the *Letter* written by Pope John Paul II to celebrate the
     founding of the Pontifical Council for Culture in 1982, quoted in M. P.
     Gallagher's book, *Clashing Symbols: An Introduction to Faith and Culture*,
     London, Darton, Longman and Todd, 1997, p. 53.

2   A more detailed treatment of this theme can be found in Gallagher, op.
     cit. See in particular the introductory chapter entitled 'Culture as
     Cinderella', pp. 1–11, and chapters four and five, pp. 44–67.

3   Ibid., p. 7

4   Ibid., p. 9

5   A summary of the views of General Secretary of the World Council of
     Churches, Konrad Raiser, 'Gospel and Cultures', *International Review of
     Mission*, 83:331 (1994), quoted in Gallagher, op. cit., pp. 57–58. Note also
     the views of Pope John Paul II: 'Sometimes witnessing to Christ will
     mean drawing out of a culture the full meaning of its noblest intentions
     . . . At other times witnessing to Christ means challenging that culture,
     especially when the truth about the human person is under assault.'
     Quoted in Gallagher, op. cit. p. 55

6   What follows are some general reflections on inner city Dublin.
     Notwithstanding the many differences to a city such as Belfast, these
     reflections may nevertheless provide a useful point of comparison. For
     further details on a Dublin urban spirituality, see M. Byrne, *A New North
     Wall Spirit* (Dublin: Elo Press, 1998) and *Walking along with Dockland
     Mystics* (Dublin: Elo Press, 1999), and B. Flanagan, *The Spirit of the City:
     Voices from Dublin's Liberties* (Dublin: Veritas, 1999).

7   Ibid. pp. 153–156; 188–190.

PART ONE

THE INNER-CITY BELFAST STORY

Listening to Inner-City Belfast Urban Voices

John Morrow
Eoin G. Cassidy

TO GET A SENSE of the positive as well as negative aspects of inner-city urban Belfast society, and the way in which these cultural factors impact on the gospel values, the working party, at an early stage, engaged in a process of listening to urban voices from both the Protestant and Catholic communities. Forty-six people agreed to be interviewed. These were roughly divided between men and women. Twenty-eight were Catholic and eighteen were Protestant, and thirty-eight were middle age or older and eight were under thirty. Clearly, this is not a representative survey, but rather a small sample of urban voices. Their views on faith in a Belfast urban environment are nonetheless worthy of recording. The reflections of these inner city residents can be grouped under three broad headings:
- What shapes peoples lives
- Faith in the light of personal attitudes and struggles
- Perception of the Church

What shapes peoples lives in inner-city Belfast?
Looking at the positive features of their lives and culture, including sources of support, most of the respondents crossing both denominational and gender boundaries focused on the experience of a close knit community, in many cases one born out of a shared sense of alienation. Most people still look to family or friends for support, although a tendency to lean on alcohol at times of stress is

evident. In some cases the support of community workers is stressed and occasionally the support of a priest, pastor, or church workers was mentioned. The dominant motivation in the life of women was, not unnaturally, the care and concern for their children. Many people seem to be living out of the spiritual capital of a grandmother or parent where deep values have been inculcated, but there is no longer a connection with a faith-community. When asked about the negative features of their lives and culture the answers were lengthier and produced some difference of emphasis between men and women and those over and under thirty years of age. Interestingly, there was practically no discernable difference between Protestant and Catholic respondents irrespective of age and gender.

The destructive influence of paramilitaries, the insular nature of their community, the scourge of drug abuse and poverty linked to unemployment and single parent families were uppermost in the minds of most women. Other issues that concerned them included alcohol abuse, violence in the home, the lack of social meeting places and poor shopping facilities. While acknowledging the destructiveness of drugs, alcohol and violence, and the negative affects of living in a ghetto community, some of the male respondents stressed the destructive effects of a growing culture of dependence that attends unemployment. They also acknowledged the negative affects of institutional sectarianism. The under-thirty category of respondents laid particular stress on the negative affects of drugs that is in many cases caused by the lack of any sense of meaning in life. Sources of authority, in particular the police, and in some cases the paramilitaries, were perceived as negative factors in their lives, although in some cases, the paramilitaries were perceived as a positive role model. In other respects their answers mirrored those of the older generation, although they laid particular stress on the lack of support for single-parent families and the lack of appropriate educational skills.

Faith in their personal lives and struggles
The questions asked under this rubric were designed to explore the faith dimension of life in the context of felt needs and desires. When asked about the sources of personal happiness, few of the

respondents stressed the religious or faith dimension of their lives. As in the answers to the previous set of questions, there was no discernible difference between Protestant and Catholic respondents. There was, however, some difference in emphasis between men and women and between those over thirty and those under thirty. The women laid particular stress on a peaceful happy family. They also mentioned freedom and financial security. Some of the men laid emphasis on community work, whereas many in the under-thirty age bracket simply spoke of having a good time. When asked about the sources of sadness or personal struggles in their lives, the women interviewed stressed marital violence or simply the lack of peace in the home. The lack of appropriate education was also mentioned. The men spoke of the debilitating effects of unnecessary disputes and the under thirties laid particular stress on the annoyance caused by structures of authority or power, from whatever source. They also spoke of the personal difficulties caused by violence in the home and the lack of appropriate education for life.

Reality of religious faith?

The more specific questions about the reality of religious faith in their personal lives elicited responses that showed some differences of emphasis. Responses from those of a Protestant background suggested that whereas belief in God was generally accepted, its connection to the everyday struggles of life and its link with Church is extremely tenuous. Some respondents spoke of the importance of Christian values and the Sunday school. One respondent spoke of the difficulty of being accepted as a Christian worker, noting that the term Christian is often a handicap both in the work place and in the community. By and large, the Catholic respondents showed a greater sense of awareness of the importance of faith in their daily lives, stressing the importance of prayer and a sense that God is the only one who can be depended upon. Furthermore, the answers offered by the Catholic respondents suggest that, for better or worse, religious faith is closely bound up with their experience of the local priest or member of religious order, respondents giving examples of how positive or negative encounters with them have affected their religious faith. However, the contrast with the Protestant experience should not be exaggerated. There is some evidence that among the Catholic respondents the connection between personal faith and attendance at Sunday mass is as tenuous as that observed from the Protestant respondents. When asked about their image of God, Protestants were more likely to answer in terms of the image of a saviour whereas Catholics were more likely to see God as a father – caring but also a disciplinarian.

Perceptions of the Church

As one might expect, perceptions varied between the different denominations – but only by way of emphasis. The reaction to questions about their Church from all respondents irrespective of religious affiliation was overwhelmingly critical. Many non-churchgoers still sent their children for Baptism and to Sunday School, but they rarely became active church members. Reasons given for non-attendance (which may not touch the heart of the matter) were boring services; laziness; baptism refused; former youth club resentments, etc. Church Services were criticised for lack of lively music; buildings were often said to be inaccessible and not open for community activities. Protestants spoke of the Church and church ministers being distant from the lives and concerns of people – particularly those who felt estranged from church affiliation. A typical comment is the following, 'the minister should be part of everyday life in the community, and he should not just be there for the church members but for the people outside the church that really need him'. There was the feeling expressed by some Protestants that Catholic priests were more in touch with their local community than Protestant ministers. While some expressed the view that the Church is the congregation, others spoke of the institutional character of the Church and made the point that concern with tradition and the maintenance of the symbols of the institution contributed to the perceived failure of the church to connect with people's lives. Although some respondents recognised that part of the purpose of the Church is to praise God, nevertheless, when asked questions that touched on the importance of worship, the feeling was expressed that worship doesn't meet the needs of

Christians, let alone those who class themselves as being outside the church. Church services are seen as boring.

If responses from the Protestant respondents suggested a sense of the irrelevance of the Church, those from the Catholic community suggested rather the power of the Church and specifically unwillingness on the part of the Church to share power with the lay members of the Church or to support initiatives from this quarter. Typical comments were as follows, 'the hierarchy is unwilling to hear the voice of the laity – they are fearful of giving up power to lay people,' and 'the church is not interested in anything that they do not control.' Some respondents' views echoed those of their Protestant neighbours, namely that the Church is no longer perceived as life-giving but is rather inward looking – concerned with maintenance rather than evangelisation. However, despite some responses that echoed the view expressed by the Protestant respondents – that the Church does not connect with their lives – other responses suggested some form of identification with the Church or even the church building. One respondent spoke of the Church building being a place of sanctuary and peace – 'somewhere to go for a break'. When asked about Sunday worship, some responses suggested a growing convergence with the experience in the Protestant Churches. Some respondents suggested that people are not only no longer drawn to the Mass out of a sense of duty, but that 'they are increasingly not drawn to Mass at all'. As with some Protestant evaluations of Sunday worship, the Mass was experienced by some Catholics as boring, reflecting either the lack of a sense of community or that worship is unrelated to life issues.

Perspectives of women, men and young people

Looking at perceptions of the Church from the perspectives of women and men some interesting things emerge. Women stressed the importance of the minister or priest being a part of the everyday life of the community and whose care embraced churchgoers and non-churchgoers alike. Issues such as child abuse and the perception that the Church is not a listening Church also featured in their replies. When asked if they felt a part of the Church, the majority answered in the negative, some feeling not valued by the Church, others objecting to the attitude and life-style of the priests and others feeling that it is Christ not the Church who should be the object of one's allegiance. The Churches' involvement or lack of involvement in political matters also received some attention. One woman from the Catholic community felt that the Church was indifferent to the sufferings of the nationalist community, and one from the Protestant community criticised the Church's involvement with the Orange order. Some Catholic women criticised the Church's negative attitudes to mixed marriage and integrated schools. There was also a strong demand for more adult catechism from some of the more articulate women.

The viewpoints of men largely echoed those of women. They laid particular stress on the lack of support from the Churches for their work in the community. Some resented changes in church teaching, although this was very much a minority viewpoint and contested by many women who felt that the Churches had not kept pace with the changing times. Some respondents felt that the Churches are responsible for the continuation of the strife in Northern Ireland. The failure to dialogue with paramilitaries was felt to have aggravated the violence in the past and caused further alienation (in this regard the work of Clonard Monastery was perceived to be the exception to the rule).

The differences between the answers to these questions suggested by men and women are in some instances quite pronounced. Agnosticism, religious indifference and alienation from the Church is much more evident in the answers from the male respondents than in those received from the women. With few exceptions, those respondents from the under-thirty age bracket showed no evidence that religious faith was a positive influence in their daily lives. God was absent and not missed. Many stressed that the Church is simply irrelevant and that Church buildings hold no attraction. Reasons given for the perceived irrelevance of the Church vary, but they largely focus on the belief that the Church is not a listening Church and that in particular, the Church has little time for young people. The scandal of child abuse was also mentioned as a contributory factor in young people's sense of alienation from the Church. A few of the responses from this age cohort, however, suggested either directly or indirectly that a loss of confidence in God's presence carried with it a loss of hope in anything or anybody. Wherever these young respondents felt some sense of identity with the Church it was either because of a positive encounter with some priest or minister or a strong upbringing in the faith from an early age.

Reflecting on the interviews

One of the most interesting of the findings from this small gathering of inner city Belfast voices is the close correlation between the descriptions of social deprivation among those over the age of thirty. In this respect, gender or denominational differences seem to be less pronounced than those based on age. When it came to describing the reality of faith in their daily lives the same patterns emerged, all the more surprising, given the polarization of the communities along religious lines. With few exceptions, belief in God was acknowledged as a positive reality in their lives, although this was much less evident in the responses from those aged under thirty. In nearly every case, however, belief in God was situated in a relation of opposition to either a belief in, or contact with, their respective Churches. Many of the reasons given for this negative view of Church were also shared by both Catholics and Protestants. These included the absence of any sense of the Church as a listening Church, and the view that Churches are more concerned with maintaining their structures than with giving value and meaning to new ways of expressing belief.

Some significant differences in Protestant and Catholic attitudes

Obviously there are some significant differences between the broad range of mainstream Protestant opinion and Catholic attitudes to their respective Churches. There was an interesting tendency among Protestants to emphasise the need to 'sort out one's own problems' rather than foist them on others, a kind of individualism, which probably has both positive and negative aspects. The latter aspect could possibly be seen in the views expressed by some Protestant respondents that the Church was irrelevant to their lives. This contrasted with Catholics whose responses offered less evidence that the Church is irrelevant. Responses from Catholics rather tended both to emphasise and to be particularly critical of the power of the Church – a resentment of the use of power to control people or to make moral judgements. There was also the perceived unwillingness on the part of the Catholic Church to give a voice to lay people, i.e. lack of partnership in ministry. Regarding this issue of power and inclusivity, it could be argued that the democratic character of Church leadership that is a feature of many Protestant communities, particularly in the Presbyterian Church, moderates the full force of this criticism that is levelled at the Catholic Church. Working-class criticism of Protestant Churches is more likely to be expressed in terms of indifference and less so as authoritarianism.

What must be recognised is that the suggested irrelevance of the mainstream Protestant Churches to many inner city residents cannot be too easily equated with religious indifference – witness the significant growth in Belfast of the Pentecostal sects, and, in particular, the growth of Pastor McConnell's Metropolitan Tabernacle. Indeed, there is some evidence to suggest that many of those who remain religious in the increasingly secular culture that is Belfast have shifted from mainstream Protestantism to these Pentecostal sects. Perhaps they find in these newer Pentecostal or Evangelical churches an ethos that is more in tune with their culture, i.e. churches that are more concerned with feelings and the therapeutic than with doctrine and beliefs. If this is the case, it is not something that is confined to Belfast but merely reflects trends evident throughout the western world. Indeed, in many South American countries there is evidence of a shift in allegiance among some Catholics to the Evangelical and Pentecostal sects. It may be the case that some of these Pentecostal churches pander to a kind of sentimentalism and to a rather simplistic fundamentalist theology that carries a superficial attraction, providing a rather questionable criteria for 'success' that is easily measurable in terms of material prosperity. However, this shift in allegiance of Catholics to the Pentecostal Churches is clearly not replicated in Belfast. This is undoubtedly the case because current communal divisions in Belfast would make this shift culturally impossible even if it were to be perceived as attractive from a religious point of view.

Geographical parishes and commuter Churches

Inner city perceptions of the irrelevance of the mainstream Protestant Churches could also be partially explained by the fact that there are many people in the Protestant/Loyalist community who have had no contact with their church for up to three generations. Alienation from the institutional church in the Roman Catholic areas of inner city Belfast is perhaps a more recent phenomenon. There is another significant difference between the Loyalist/Protestant and Republican or Nationalist/Catholic communities in Belfast that touches upon the nature of the parish or congregation. In Catholic areas parish communities have a strong geographical focus, and, in consequence, the local priest has strong links with the local community and not just the church-going public. This is less evident in Protestant areas where there is often, though not always, a clear distinction between the congregational community and the community who live adjacent to the church or meeting hall. This is a phenomenon that has given rise to the concept of commuter parishes. In this context, there is a question as to whether there is a connection between the perceived irrelevance of the church and the lack of a close contact between the minister and the members of the congregational church with the local community. One should not underestimate the importance attached in Protestant culture to the idea of the church as something separate from everyday life. There is always a creative tension between the call to social and cultural solidarity and the call to be a witness to an alternative way of life that challenges the spirit of the age, in the name of Jesus Christ. This is heightened within the Protestant psyche by the emphasis in many of the denominations of individual choice of Jesus as personal Saviour. While Catholics could identify with the need to respect the tension between embracing and critiquing culture, nevertheless, the sacramental character of everyday religious observance in the Catholic Church has tended to offer a structure that links everyday life to the church in a manner that may not be as evident in the Protestant culture.

There may be a possible link between the uncertainties thrown up by living in a post-modern culture and an awareness that the questions facing many people are not being heard or recognised by

Churches, which are holding fast to answers that gave meaning to life at a different time. Yet this picture is not one of complete doom and gloom, there is much evidence to suggest that if formal religion has declined, a sense of human spirituality is alive and well. Many people are anxious to pick and choose from among the plurality of world religions and from new-age practices. At all levels of society, people are increasingly struggling with questions of meaning and purpose, which can present to the church a new opportunity of mission and service.

Culture and Alienation from Church in Working-Class Loyalism and Republicanism / Nationalism

INTRODUCTION: MODERNITY AND POST-MODERNITY IN AN URBAN CULTURE[1]

John Morrow, Eoin G. Cassidy

ONE WAY of reflecting on contemporary urban culture is to situate it in the context of a comparison between the values of the culture of modernity and what is perceived to be emerging in contemporary western culture, namely postmodernity. The following is a standard way of attempting to make this comparison.

Modernism	Postmodernism
Producer orientated	Consumer orientated
Industrial society	Technological society
Universal society	Global society
Truth is objective	All truth is interpretative
An orientation to the future	An orientation to present moment
A sense of progress	Choices / Fragmentation / Relativism
A secular world view	Religious and secular pluralism

There are some grounds for the belief that in this generation we are witnessing a cultural change that can be categorised in the manner of the tables above. While the contrast ought not be exaggerated, there is evidence that in today's urban culture people like to pick and choose and don't belong to anything for life. Furthermore, very often jobs are short term, so commitment is limited. Truth is relativised and people are inclined to a 'pick and mix' approach or to a vague scepticism about everything. On the other hand some of the modern atheistic dogmas are less fashionable and people are more willing to evaluate theories on a more pragmatic basis – do they work?

As a method for understanding the complexity of an inner-city urban culture, however, this model has its limitations. Undoubtedly, one of the most important features of contemporary urban society is its fluidity, as people cross cultural and social boundaries. This is greatly assisted by the influence of television, which works to create its own global village. Nevertheless, it must be recognised that there are equally strong factors working in the opposite direction that would question the assumption of a widespread acceptance of post-modernism in a society such as inner urban Belfast. Firstly, there is the fact that inner urban communities are very conscious of their geographical locality and in many cases define themselves in terms of belonging to a particular locality. Furthermore, there is another factor that is specific to a city such as Belfast with a history of communal tension, namely the sense of isolation or a ghetto mentality created and sustained by this tension. One does not have to be very perceptive to recognise that the idea of a global village is not one that is likely to be readily embraced by those who perceive their cultural identity to be under threat.

Another way of examining a particular culture is to look at it under four well-established headings, namely its *symbols, world views, ethos* and *social realities*.

Symbols
In the polarised inner city of Belfast or some housing estates the most prominent symbols are often sectarian tricolours or Union Jacks; paramilitary murals; football teams like Celtic or Rangers; lists of martyrs, etc. There are some signs of more hopeful graffiti such as 'Compromise or Conflict?' coming out of the peace process, but also signs of resistance to the decommissioning of paramilitary explosives, i.e. 'Not an ounce'.

World-view
With regard to the inner city and socially disadvantaged housing estates in Belfast, the world-view often appears to be very narrow

and restricted – a world-view reinforced by the sense of being under siege. The cumulative effect of communal strife and changing work patterns in Belfast has also led to a sense of fragmentation, the loss of secure boundaries that provided the building bricks of a stable world-view. Under the influence of the mass media there is exposure to a global world-view, one shaped in no uncertain way by values operative in the USA. This creates pressures that question the narrow and restricted world-view of socially disadvantaged urban areas of Belfast. The conflict between two very different world-views can contribute to a loss of identity or a conflict between the generations as to what constitutes the identity of such urban residents – a younger generation will perhaps be less willing to allow themselves to be defined in terms of the religious or cultural labels that are closely identified in terms of the communal strife in Belfast. The extent of this youthful rejection of a narrow, restricted world-view should not be exaggerated. Many inner city Belfast youths seem only too willing to embrace the siege mentality.

Ethos

The ethos of Belfast is sometimes one of confusion and lack of ownership by people of their own community. This is possibly less evident in the Nationalist areas due to increased recognition of Irishness. The contemporary achievement culture, sustained by an educated middle class, has left the poorer urban dweller disempowered and feeling unable to compete. This is often aggravated by the 11+ school selection system operative in Northern Ireland, which can make people feel a failure from an early age. This in turn engenders apathy, reflecting a lack of self-esteem and a fatalistic attitude to future progress.

Social realities

In the inner urban structure there are serious social and economic problems such as the high unemployment of unskilled people, poor housing (although in some cases this has greatly improved) and a climate of fear induced by the lack of policing and the violence of paramilitaries. There is much evidence that the abuse of alcohol and more recently drugs brings misery to many inner city families.

Furthermore, domestic violence would seem to be widespread and most areas of the inner city have a high percentage of single parents.

* * *

LOYALISM, CULTURE AND FAITH
Bill Moore

Loyalism is all-pervasive, penetrating every nook and cranny and colouring all the thought processes of those who call themselves both Loyalist and Protestant. They want it thus. It is not seen as some sort of 'affliction', this is a culture they positively strive for and nurture. What follows is a snapshot that records some of the ideals and symbols of Belfast Loyalism.

Education
Loyalists do not want integrated education. Although they will criticise the government for funding separate Roman Catholic/Protestant schools, very seldom will Loyalists avail themselves of the opportunity for integrated education. Part of the reasoning is the fear of mixed marriages – a legitimate fear if such a marriage is anathema.

It is difficult to ascertain the real attitude to languages among Loyalists. Many middle-class Protestants feel that Ulster-Scots is a macabre joke developed to continue the division in the community. Certainly there has been no rush amongst Loyalists to enroll in classes. It is perceived among Loyalists as similar to the Gaelic language on the Republican side, i.e. that it is part of the whole cultural/political matrix.

Art
Both of the working class communities have shown a talent for street painting – both the kerbs and the gable walls. Although it could be argued that Loyalists were the originators of street painting with the King Billy murals, Loyalists believe that the Republicans

have developed this into a highly effective propaganda art form. Not for either side the intellectual arguments about art for arts sake – this is art for a purpose, and if the message is not 'in your face' then it has failed. Subtlety is not highly regarded!

Another vehicle for propaganda is the performing arts. Loyalists feel inferior in the realm of performing arts and always believe that film and television documentaries are biased in favour of Catholics. Whilst not having an everyday music culture of a distinctive kind except British 'pop', and whilst having a grudging admiration for the Irish songs and dancing, the Loyalist nevertheless avoids anything that has an affinity with a Gaelic or Irish music culture. In regard to sculpture, Loyalists perceive themselves as playing 'catch up' with the Republican community and are now encouraging artists in their community to express their 'culture' through three-dimensional art.

Cultural Symbols

- *Sport:* Apart from the soccer/gaelic divisions, there are also specific teams that Loyalists claim as their own – Linfield (local), Glasgow Rangers (Scottish) and Liverpool (English). Interestingly, Glentoran is not on this list even though it originated in a Protestant area and was also perceived as a 'Protestant' team.
- *Money:* At one stage, before the currencies were finally separated, Loyalists would not use Republic of Ireland coinage and, even today, some would not go over the border to spend money.
- *Colours:* Even colour schemes are subject to Loyalist thinking. I know of one man who would not 'allow' his wife to wear green! Home decoration is with flags and bunting. I am one of the few who wears a green anorak in my parish. It is my favourite colour. I did have a lovely summer shirt with green white and rust/brown trimmings, which I never wore except on holiday.
- *Holidays:* Ballyhalbert is a favourite venue for Loyalists and is known as Little Sandy Row. Newcastle in County Down and the northeast Antrim Coast (Cushendall and the Glens) are regarded as out of bounds for Loyalists, although the north coast is quite acceptable. As a destination for holidays Scotland is preferred to England.
- *Reading:* Loyalists read the *Newsletter* although they prefer the *Star*

(Scottish). English papers are read. Irish papers are never read.

Religion

Religion must have an anti-Catholic content. Loyalists believe that the established churches that engage in mediation work with Catholics are traitorous. Ministers should not meddle in politics (a Democratic Unionist Party statement to me on one occasion!), i.e. unless they support our view! Loyalists believe in submitting to the authorities – so long as they are on our side, following our agenda. Most Loyalists believe in a God – their own God. In many cases, freedom of thought has resulted in a total indiscipline of thought. For example, to the mind of many Loyalists, the doctrine of Grace that is the cornerstone of the Protestant faith would stop short of allowing for the possibility of salvation for a leading Catholic Republican such as Gerry Adams. Loyalists are strong on Christ but weak on the hard sayings such as forgiveness of enemies or reconciliation. Many Loyalists would say prayers on a daily basis. The Lord's Prayer, however, must present grave problems, considering that it includes the Christian teaching on forgiving as we are forgiven. The rendering of the authorised version (King James AD 1611) softens it with 'forgive as we forgive'. This does not have the same impact as 'forgive the same way as we forgive' (*Good News*).

In the light of Loyalist interpretation of the Christian faith, the task for the Protestant Churches is to reinterpret God for Loyalists in a manner that is compatible with the tenets of the Christian faith. This will have to start all over again with children. The responsibility on each one of us to 'be Christ' (and thus reinterpret God) in our local situation is awesome and may account for the high health toll on ministers of religion in the 'working class' Protestant communities.

* * *

Republicanism/Nationalism, Culture and Faith
Patrick McCafferty

An elected representative said to me recently that, for many people in working-class Nationalist communities, the philosophy, culture and symbols of Irish Republicanism have replaced the Church and religious faith. There is a great deal of truth in his observation and for many reasons.

Street art celebrating icons of the Republican struggle and the ideals they represent adorn working class areas. For many people now, the crucial definition of their identity is not that they are Catholic but that they are Nationalist/Republican. Nationalists take a very strong pride in every aspect of Irish culture and heritage.

A whole new liberation of the working class community has evolved with many extremely intelligent and articulate spokespersons. There has been an upsurge in creative energy finding expression in the visual and performing arts, resulting in very powerful and vivid evocations of the last four pain-filled decades of the twentieth century.

There is a whole new dimension to the Irish identity emerging that is almost completely disengaged from 'religion'. Paradoxically, the Irish language itself, which is so replete with references to God and spiritual realities, has, in many parts of Belfast, become attractive to people who are distant from the Church. In some cases, people are opting to educate their children through the medium of Irish precisely because Irish-speaking schools have no association with the Catholic Church and are intended to be non-denominational. Also, a growing percentage of working class families are beginning to send their children to integrated schools.

Among the urban Nationalist working class, there is virtually no antipathy towards the Protestant Churches – their beliefs, theologies and worship. There is no reciprocation of the intense suspicion and virulent hatred of Catholicism as a religious system that is still quite strong among Protestants. Nationalist/Republicans, for example, do not regard the Moderator of the Presbyterian Church as 'the Antichrist'; nor do they denounce the Church of Ireland as 'the

Whore of Babylon'. Furthermore, there is surprisingly little bitterness towards ordinary working class Protestant people as such. Many atrocities were committed against working class Nationalists by Loyalist paramilitaries from similar backgrounds. In spite of this, the real villain of the piece is always Britain and the wealthy and privileged Unionist establishment that held power and bolstered up the system of discrimination and injustice.

Nationalists reserve their extreme animosity for all that constitutes and represents 'Britishness'. There is a profound distrust, resentment and, frequently, outright hatred of the British State. Nationalists see red at any reference to the North of Ireland as part of the 'United Kingdom' and the implication of themselves as 'British subjects' – a revolting term – because it is so evocative of our subjugation and brutalisation as a people throughout history and in very recent times.

Catholic working-class communities bore the brunt of the merciless might of the British Army and they regard the RUC (Royal Ulster Constabulary) as the gun-toting wing of Ulster Unionism. Many working class families lost loved ones as a result of indiscriminate force exercised by armed Security Forces. These people never received justice or even any sense of their grievances being taken seriously by the British and Unionist establishment. Consequently, there is still very little openness to the stories of pain and loss that members of the Security Forces and their families also have to tell.

For Catholics/Nationalists, the link with Britain is fraught with difficulty, but a relationship exists nonetheless. For example, working-class Catholics are coming to realise that their struggles for survival have much in common with similar communities in Manchester, London, Birmingham and Glasgow. Nationalists mainly read the *Irish News* and the *Andersonstown News*, though the British tabloids are also widely read, and the British television serials (soaps) are equally popular. Alongside the traditional support for Celtic and Cliftonville, there is widespread support for soccer teams such as Manchester United and Liverpool. Needless to say, the GAA (Gaelic Athletic Association) is also quite strong.

The Nationalist/Republican working class seems to be more outward looking than their Loyalist/Unionist counterparts. There is openness to other cultures across the world. Connections have developed, for example, with Basques and Native Americans. This global perspective, hopefully, will help put Ireland's troubles into a more universal context and bear fruit at local level. One of the major problems facing us, in working class communities across the so-called divide, is that people literally living a stones throw from one another might as well live a thousand miles apart.

In many working-class districts, religious practice is less than ten per cent and falling. There is alienation from the institutional Church and, for an increasing number, 'religion', as experienced until now, is irrelevant and unappealing. Working-class people dislike Church officialdom and don't trust the hierarchy. Many report very bad experiences at the hands of Church personnel. They perceive the institutional Church as having behaved treacherously towards its own people. At the same time, there is a persistent faith in God and many people who don't come to church continue to have real relationships with God.

In the Catholic working-class community, it is sometimes more accurate to speak of the 'dis-churched' rather than the 'un-churched'. There are many people who have had a very negative experience of Church in their upbringing and who have subsequently walked away from the human institution. Nevertheless, they will continue to have devotion to someone like Blessed Padre Pio – a priest whom they understand as having had time for everyone.

The death-knell is sounding, louder and louder, for a way of being Church that has now resulted in the estrangement of many working-class people. They are not coming back to the Church, so the Church better do what Jesus did – setting out into all those places where His hurting and alienated people have been scattered. No longer a brutal, power-abusing Church, which was little different from people's lived experience in the political reality but the real Church of the One who searches for people, who finds them in their pain and brokenness and who tenderly lifts them up and, rejoicing, carries them home.

Notes

1   In preparing this short article we wish to acknowledge the contribution
     of the Rev. John Harvey, former leader of the Iona community.

Belfast Urban Faith Stories

INTRODUCTION: SHARING OUR STORIES
Eoin G. Cassidy

STORY, OR NARRATIVE, shapes human culture and identity. We are who we are because of the stories that we hold in common. 'Our lives are ceaselessly intertwined with narrative, with the stories that we tell and hear told, those we dream or imagine or would like to tell, all of which are reworked in that story of our lives that we narrate to ourselves.'[1] Each of us is born into a web of stories about humankind in general, about certain people and about ourselves in particular and the task facing each of us is to assimilate these stories into his or her own story, a story that he or she can personally sign. However, in a society marked by diverse and, in many cases, conflicting stories, we must be acutely conscious that this task is not to be fulfilled alone, but together in dialogue with other storytellers whose stories can and do place limits on our freedom to tell stories.

For those reared in the political, social and religious turmoil that marked Belfast over the past thirty years, the importance of listening to other people's stories needs no stressing. If we are to be able to appreciate the richness of the religious and cultural tapestry that shapes contemporary urban Belfast we need to share our stories and we need to be able to hear each other's stories. To do otherwise risks living in a fantasy world that is filled with destructive potential. It is in this spirit that we have included this section in our reflections on faith in inner-city Belfast.

In the course of our work many urban stories saw the light of day. What follows is a small sample of those that were told to us. They are grouped into three sets of three stories, all of which give a flavour of the narrative character of faith as it is lived in an inner city environment:

1. Stories about Paddy told by Kathleen Keane
2. Stories from Women told by Kathy Higgins
3. Musings on urban ministry told by Ken Groves and Eddie McDowell

The three stories from Kathleen Keane tell of a person named Paddy and remind us that religious faith is always contextual. Life as a Catholic in the Springfield Road is not just any Catholic life, and the faith story of one person is never removed from the cultural context within which it is situated. The outwardly simple lifestyle of Paddy reflects a carefully honed response to the scourge of sectarianism. His kindness challenges the pervasiveness of a sectarian culture. Paddy's story is an example of Christianity lived on the peace-line. He is a peacemaker rather than a theoriser. His ministry is remarkable for its inclusivity. It is a ministry of the greeting, one that reflects the conviction that a greeting can heal divisions.

The three stories that tell of women as peacemakers likewise show us that faith is always contextual. They tell us that the gospel imperatives are prioritised in a particular context. Contemporary urban Belfast gives witness to the priority of being a peacemaker. These stories also remind us of the manner in which Christianity connects or fails to connect because of cultural factors. Contemporary culture is increasingly intolerant of institutions that are perceived to fail to recognise the equality of women and men. The stories also show the complexity of Christian witness, or how difficult it is to be the Good Samaritan when tribal loyalties take a higher priority than Christian faith. It is very difficult to break free from the cultural constraints, and the Church will have to accept that popularity is not a worthy goal.

The brief musings recorded by Ken Groves and Eddie McDowell highlight the tension in the inner cities as the Christian community struggles to understand the meaning of urban ministry. In this context, social engagement and evangelism are often separated and given different priorities, which are often reinforced by many of our religious traditions. Some would argue, however, that no such division becomes apparent when we examine scripture and the ministry of Christ. If we love our neighbour as God made him, we must inevitably be concerned for his total welfare, the good of his soul, his body and his community. The musings also raise a number of issues for the wider Christian community, such as the need to develop realistic models of ministry within urban culture, e.g. a community development approach, social engagement, the use of Church premises, etc.

* * *

STORIES ABOUT PADDY
told by Kathleen Keane

A greeting builds a village (Zimbabwean proverb)

Paddy and Mary lived on Springfield Road, when it was a leafy, desirable place to live. Gradually however, all their neighbours left, including the Protestant family in the other half of their semi-detached house. Mary cried all that day after her friend left. She and Paddy quickly found themselves attached to a derelict, vandalised house, with back and front gardens trampled over and used as dumps.

I came to live in this next-door house, after it was 'restored'. Paddy suggested to me that, whenever anyone went by my garden fence, back or front, I should say to them: 'That's a nice day today'. I rehearsed this doubtfully, in what I hoped sounded like a Belfast accent.

Our two lone houses (this meant literally having a 'Catholic' front door and a 'Protestant' back door) were part of a 'peace-line', with a high metal barrier attached to the side of each house. The pedestrian gate through the barrier was locked every night and anytime there was any 'trouble'. When this happened people would ring my doorbell, asking to pass through the house. Or, from the back, they would come to the kitchen door, asking to go out onto Springfield

Road, again walking through the house. 'That's a nice day,' I said to everyone. And it worked; I began to make some real friends.

In the summertime, Paddy seemed to be in this front garden a lot, most often leaning on his hoe, talking to some passer-by. He told me that the hoe was an excuse for his real intention – getting people to talk to him. When he could not pretend anymore to be gardening, because there wasn't a weed in sight, he would come into my garden and 'work', with the same ulterior motive of putting chat on the passers-by.

With his encouragement and some effort from me, my garden bloomed again. To prove that other things, besides stones, could cross Springfield Road, a man across the way gave me a slip of his large pink mallow plant. Under Paddy's planting instructions, it grew so big beside my house that it filled the empty space in front of the barrier where my side-garden should have been.

Over the years some passers-by refused to meet my eyes, much less agree that it was a nice day; a few hurried past with eyes averted, and having missed the instant of eye-contact, I did not have the courage to greet them. Most, however, smiled and returned the weather talk; eventually people began to stop, admire the flowers and have a little chat. And yet Paddy had never heard the African proverb: 'A greeting builds a village'.

Before the local peace line was built, the Whiterock Orange Parade used to come onto Springfield Road through Coupar Street and was sometimes subjected to stoning and other resistance measures. After such an episode, as the parade moved up Springfield Road, through what was still a mixed area, various sympathisers would minister to any 'walking wounded' – casualties of the stones.

From his vantage point at the front gate, Paddy saw that one Orangeman with a head wound had blood staining his shirt. Forthwith he invited him into the house and up to the bathroom to clean up. Not only that, but he gave him a good shirt of his own, in which to continue the parade, much to Mary's chargin. She had bought him that shirt shortly before.

However, she had an unsought distraction of her own to deal with. A woman acquaintance of the Orangeman, who had been following the parade, followed him into the house and asked Mary for a drink of water. Presuming that she was in a Protestant house, this woman began to complain in colourful language about the '. . . Fenians'. She complained that the previous parade had been stoned in Ardoyne and now again in Clonard.

Mary was speechless and was preoccupied with hanging a tea towel over her Beleek holy water font, before the woman would see it. She made a mental note to keep Paddy away from the front gate – if possible.

Sport: cultural variety

Paddy enjoyed all sport; and even a new neighbour, who knew nothing about sport, was no problem for him. Our back gardens had a gate between them and I soon wore a little track to Mary and Paddy's backdoor. If he was watching sport on television he would politely turn the sound off and that way, we could all talk and he could keep an eye on the action, whatever it was. I never felt that I was getting second-class attention.

Both Mary and Paddy talked nostalgically of a time when 'everyone' went up Workman Avenue to the bowling green in Woodvale Park. Protestants and Catholics also enjoyed summer evening drinks together at the pub across the Springfield Road. Now that side of the road is a residential nationalist area. I try in vain to imagine it as a 'mixed' area and to visualise a different Springfield road with a garage, post office, all kinds of shops and even a bank.

Cricket or tennis over, Paddy would switch to 'Gaelic' or golf, snooker, or any of the inexplicable sporting pastimes beloved by men. *All* kinds formed a backdrop to Paddy's fund of stories. His nature, however, for all this seemed to hold no competitiveness; he was trying to prove nothing, except that good relations were for the good and enjoyment of all.

Paddy was a great reader too; books and papers crossed the back gate in both directions regularly. Half-price Sunday newspapers from the garage on Lanark Way were good while they lasted. In a cease-fire era, this garage was the first and only thing to come back to life in the no man's land between the Shankill and Springfield roads. Once I grumbled to Paddy about some English broadsheet journalist, who did not seem to quite understand some aspect of our troubled peace.

'And who does understand it?' Paddy replied. 'Look how long you are here and you don't understand it'

'I know,' I replied irritably, 'but I know that I don't understand it.'

Paddy's hearty laugh ringing across the peace-line was a feature of those days and nights. He treasured what he held in common with all the people of his own province, but would also generously 'educate' a southerner who understood hardly anything about Northern Ireland. Southerners, like everyone else, were sure of a welcome.

Enjoyment of difference

Paddy loved variety – anyone or anything different fascinated him. His working life had been spent with a drinks firm and publicans across all areas of Belfast liked, respected and 'looked out' for him. A salesman during 'the Troubles' needed such consideration at times and Paddy was appreciative of many favours and friendships. It offended his soul that there was also bitter and lethal division in his city.

In midsummer, his garden ablaze with a splendid variety of roses, Paddy, now retired, leaned on his gate with his dog Ben by his side. One day a serious young woman-tourist approached up the road. Obviously foreign, she gazed at the peace wall and the huge, ugly, metal barrier. Encouraged by Paddy's greeting, she stopped and her first words were a question about the function of the peace-line.

Bluntly Paddy said: 'That's there because two sets of Christians cannot live with each other'.

And the earnest young woman replied: 'But a wall will not work either and it will be knocked down, just as in my country, it has been knocked down.'

Her short life experience, which made her so confident, seemed to speak to Paddy's long endurance of violence and division. He was afterwards fond of quoting this young woman, whom he found so convincing, in relation to his own hopes and dreams. While he loved variety and enjoyed the best elements of both Republicanism and Royalism, he hated division. With Ben beside him he would stand at the front gate greeting and chatting to passersby, whether Catholic or Protestant, men or women, soldiers, police, tourists, journalists,

Orangemen or total strangers, everyone got a friendly: 'Nice day today'.

Ben provided an attraction in himself with his thick, rough Kerry-blue coat. Another feature of his was that his two front teeth protruded in what looked like a smile. He had acquired this 'expression' through an incurable habit of crossing and re-crossing Springfield Road. Inevitably one day, he was knocked down for his anti-sectarianism. He recovered slowly from his injuries, with the love and care of Paddy and Mary. The latter fed him spoonfuls of whiskey 'for the pain' while he was still wearing his conspicuous 'surgical' collar.

As Ben improved, Mary would lift his front paws onto their usual position on the first bar of the gate, so that he could again view life on the road, as he loved to do. Long after the collar went, Ben 'smiled' engagingly at all and sundry, as if imitating his master.

* * *

Stories from Women
told by Kathy Higgins

Women as peacemakers in Belfast

As examples of peacemaking in Northern Ireland, I shall relate some of the experiences told to me by two women, Baroness May Blood and Mary Lavery, who are Protestant and Catholic respectively, and from similar socio-economic areas in Belfast.

May shared two memories that fuelled her desire to work for peace. In the early 70s, May had been living in a mixed area in West Belfast, although, she recalls, in one weekend all this changed. The underlying anger, suspicion and hatred between a number of the Protestants and Catholics in the area exploded following a local Orange Parade, and there was a real danger that lives would be lost and homes destroyed. A number of Catholic and Protestant women came together and decided the only way to ensure the safety of their families was to residentially segregate the area. They renegotiated the boundaries creating two separate ghettos, one Catholic the other Protestant, and swapped their houses helping each other move. This action averted what could have been a real atrocity. The mill May worked in was situated in Catholic West Belfast. On one occasion, returning from work, she came upon a young Catholic boy writing a slogan on a wall, it read 'Is there life before death?' May realised the child perceived no future for himself and this goaded her to work toward creating a better future for the sake of the children.

Mary's decision to work for peace had its roots in her experiences during the Hunger Strike in the early 80s. As a mother, she wondered how she would react if her son had chosen to starve himself to death; she decided to channel her anger at the waste of human life into working for peace. Through Cornerstone, an ecumenical community situated in Catholic West Belfast, she made contact with a number of Protestant women living on the other side of the peace-wall, erected to keep the two communities apart. Many of these women were mothers who, Mary discovered, shared a similar fear to her own, that their sons might become involved with the paramilitaries. As they shared their fears and struggles to hold onto some semblance of normality amidst the ongoing riots and shootings, a bond developed between them.

The contributions of women to peacemaking in Northern Ireland will never be fully known. The sacrifices and risks undertaken by many women in the past are beginning to bear fruit in this new century. Women, like May and Mary, who continue to work tirelessly for peace to ensure the youth of today have a future, are reminders to us that 'there can be no peace for any of us until there is peace for us all.'

Women in the shadow of the peace-line
A large brick wall runs along part of the Springfield Road as a solid reminder of the hostility, fear and violence that has infected those communities living on either side of it. The belief is that without the protection the wall offered, from those on the other side, the survival of both communities would be threatened.

Women, living on both sides of the so-called peace-line in West Belfast, have struggled to hold family and community together over the last 30 years of civil unrest. I spoke with a number of Catholic and Protestant women from this area that participated in one of the Irish School of Ecumenics adult education programmes. What struck me was the similarity of their experiences and perceptions.

When asked about their faith, the women were unanimous in stressing the centrality of it to their lives. When violence erupted onto the streets and they lived in fear of any member of their family being harmed, or if their husbands or sons were late home and they were unsure of their whereabouts, it was their belief in God that sustained them. Some expressed the view that it was their faith in a future, different from the present, based on God's justice, peace and compassion that fuelled their attempts to hold the community together. It also spurred them on to care for the needs of the young people, elderly, disabled and sick who were the most vulnerable within their communities.

I asked if this compassion and generosity of spirit was extended to those whom they consider the 'enemy' living across the peace-line? Some admitted that they felt they were the 'victims' in the war. They believed that whatever ill treatment the other community experienced, they had brought it on themselves. Other women admitted that they had known families living 'on the other side' before the 'troubles' and although they were concerned for their safety, they had no way of discovering how they were coping.

Where, I put it to them, did they see God in all of this? There was a clear sense that each believed God was with them, protecting them, on their side as it were. We then spent some time reflecting on how and why their attitudes toward each other had changed. It became apparent as the conversation progressed that it was through sharing their experiences of fear and vulnerability and their struggles to protect themselves and their families that relationships between them developed. The opportunities to listen to, hear and acknowledge the truth of the other enabled them to recognise the humanness of the other. They found themselves, consequently, not only sharing their dreams of a better future for their children but also working together to put flesh on those dreams.

Although all of the women in the group attended their respective churches and actively supported them, they, in general, shared a sense of being let down and abandoned by their churches. Both the Protestant and Catholic women believed their churches had failed them throughout the Troubles. For the most part, individual churchmen refused to challenge those who were encouraging the youth to riot and vandalise property. The perception was that they did not wish to be associated with any of the paramilitary groupings. In choosing not to engage with them, however, they were perceived as opting out.

It was acknowledged that individual clergymen did what they could to minister to the injured and bereaved. When asked how they felt about those clergy who crossed the peace-line to comfort families suffering on the other side, there was a general feeling that they were viewed with suspicion and charged with being more concerned with the needs of the other community.

As they further reflected on their experience of church now, many of the women expressed a sense of dissatisfaction. When we explored what was at the root of this feeling, it emerged that many of them resented the role that was ascribed to them in church, that of making tea and offering hospitality. Although they saw this as important, they also wished to have more of a say in decision making within their churches. One woman explained that it was left to the women to take control of their communities, when many of the men were not available because they were either in hiding, imprisoned, injured or killed. During that time, the women had shown themselves capable of giving leadership and had succeeded in holding the fabric of their community together at difficult and dangerous moments. Through their actions, the women had come to a greater sense of what they could contribute to the wider community.

I asked the women to reflect on the type of leadership they expected from their churches. In response, some indicated that they were of the opinion that a good leader is in touch with and concerned about people in the community, and has an ability to address the issues and problems they are struggling with on a daily basis. Those with responsibility for leadership in the local churches, they felt, needed to really engage with the people, so that a way could be found to bring the 'Good News' into conversation with the realities of our time.

Others made the point that a good leader empowers others to use their own gifts in the service of God and the community. The model of shared leadership that the women fostered to address the needs of their local communities, was suggested as an example of the type of leadership that could be adopted in our churches.

Are you invisible too?

As a Catholic woman living in Belfast and working in the field of reconciliation, particularly with the churches, my job brings me into contact with many women from the different Christian churches. Reflecting on my own experience of church, and listening to other women recount their experiences, I have become increasingly aware of the many women who are struggling to find nourishment within their churches. Their anger at the lack of inclusive language or appropriate biblical role models for women seemed to go unnoticed, or was dismissed, by those in positions in authority.

It has struck me forcibly that as the biblical stories about women stand, they both fit and do not fit reality as we experience it. In reading the stories of women in Scripture, we need to ask whose interests are served in the texts? What difference does it make to our understanding of the stories, if we focus on the women's experiences? Jesus associated with women and restored the dignity due them, regardless of their social status or stigma; in some instances women challenged Jesus by what they said and did. What can women living at this time and in this place learn from those women who touched Jesus' life?

Recently, in my work for the Irish School of Ecumenics, I had occasion to work with two different adult education groups, one Catholic, one Protestant, one in North Belfast and the other in the South of the City. Both groups were made up of men and women. The topic we were exploring was 'Women in the Early Christian Church'. As a prelude to exploring the issue, I asked the women in the group to say something about their experience of church. Words began to surface expressive of women's experience of invisibility. They felt overlooked, excluded, undervalued, undernourished, frustrated, angry, disempowered and unfulfilled.

Two of the stories recounted, one from each group, have stayed with me. They illustrate some of the difficulties that are preventing women from having a positive experience of church. The two women who shared their particular experience were in their mid-thirties and, although attending their church, indicated their struggles to find nourishment for their faith journeys within their church.

The first woman told the story of a woman friend of hers within her congregation, who had been chosen to take on the responsibility of elder in the church. At the service of worship, which celebrated and affirmed her friend's call to eldership within the church, the minister and other elders laid their hands on her friend to pray for her. No attempt was made to change the language in the worship service to take account of the fact that the new elder was a woman. Consequently, in their prayer, the group asked for a blessing on 'our brother in Christ'. The woman recounting the story told of her feelings of incomprehensibility and anger at the insensitivity shown toward her friend's gender identity during the service.

The second woman shared her frustration at trying to find positive biblical female role models for women to assist her in her own spiritual development. As she leafed through the Acts and Letters in the New Testament, in an attempt to find women she could relate to, she was struck by the lack of attention to women. She also commented that she had never heard a church sermon on the role of women in the early Church. Her question to me was, 'Where do I need to go to read or hear about women who would inspire me?'

What saddened me in this encounter was the lack of awareness of the roles undertaken by women in the early church. Women were active participants in all areas of the life and mission of the Christian communities. They were apostles, teachers, prophetesses, providers, workers and preachers, each according to her potential and God-given talents. If these women's stories were recovered, they could provide the necessary models to enable women today to become more proactive in their churches.

Jesus through his relationships with women, listening to them and including them in his ministry, made them visible in their own communities. Jesus took women seriously and recognised their value. If women are to recover their visibility in the churches, their stories need to be heard. Only when women's wisdom is recognised and fully appreciated will we be able to find more inclusive, life-giving ways of being church in our particular context.

✳ ✳ ✳

MUSINGS ON URBAN MINISTRY
told by Ken Groves and Eddie McDowell

A community development model

A short extract from committee meeting minutes dated June 1999: 'The secretary proposed that the organisation should fully implement a community development approach to all its activities within the local area. This was seconded and unanimously agreed by the rest of the committee. Joan raised the next motion on the agenda, a local woman who runs the women's project. It concerned their open day to be held in July of the same year. She informed the committee of the group's plan to have a cake stall, secondhand clothes stall and to have entertainment for the children. In addition to this there would be a fortuneteller and aromatherapist for the mothers. At this point the secretary stated that this was a Christian organisation and that it would be totally unacceptable to have a fortune teller and aromatherapist as both of these where biblically unacceptable. Joan then asked the committee if it had not just unanimously agreed to implement a community development model in relation to all its activities? Did this not mean empowering people to make their own choices and in relation to the open day the women's groups had made their own informed choice of what they wanted to do.'

'Faith without works is dead'

John was telling me about a debate that took place at his mid-week meeting concerning urban ministry. It was centred on the lack of leadership and limited number of people willing to help out with Church activities. One of the elders angrily quoted from scripture saying that 'faith without works is dead' and that he would have serious concerns about the commitment of a number of people within this Church, as it was the same five people who do everything. It was then pointed out by John, who managed the local hospice, that without the volunteers from this Church the hospice would most likely have closed . . .

An advice centre

A local CAB approached the Church Committee and asked if it would be possible to use the premises for their advice centre. It was pointed out by a committee member that the organist used the hall for practice on the same days required by CAB and that surely Christian activity should take precedence over secular activity . . .

Notes

1   Brooks, P., *Reading for the Plot: Design and Intention in Narrative*, New York, Vintage, 1984, p. 3.

PART TWO

THE BELFAST STORY
IN A HISTORICAL PERSPECTIVE

Religious and Social Interaction in Nineteenth- and Early Twentieth-Century Belfast

John Morrow

THE DEVELOPMENT of the industrial revolution, which led to the rapid growth of towns and cities in the nineteenth century, often rendered existing religious structures inadequate or irrelevant. David Hempton and Myrtle Hill have documented much of this in their book *Evangelical Protestantism in Ulster Society 1740-1890.*[1]

Church outreach in a growing city
Church extension programmes in the mid-nineteenth century were often too late or too limited. In Belfast some congregations resisted through fear of losing numerical or financial strength. To a considerable extent, however, religious ideas, values and symbols did permeate the popular culture. Belfast sustained rapid population growth from 32,000 in 1821 to 350,000 by 1901. Many migrated to the city in the wake of the famine and the unreliability of the potato harvest, and as a result of decline in the rural domestic linen industry. New manufacturing centers such as Belfast, switched from cotton to linen and the port was enlarged for shipping and shipbuilding.

The conditions of the inner-city poor were bad, with overcrowding and bad sanitation in tiny houses, leading to fever, disease and high mortality. The periodic depressions in the industries and in work availability produced cycles of crime, poverty and violence. The percentage of Catholics rose rapidly from eight per

cent at the turn of the century to forty per cent by 1850. Thereafter
Protestant migration increased as some Catholics migrated further
afield. The migrating Protestants were on average more skilled and
the encounter with unskilled labourers from a Catholic background
led to harsh stereotyping. Late eighteenth-century Belfast had a
more tolerant tradition with Presbyterians supporting the building
of the first Catholic church. The nineteenth century saw the
emergence of sectarian strife. Rural dwellers brought some of the
strong orange and green traditions with them from the sectarian
heartland of mid-Ulster, and this, together with other forms of social
rivalry, proved to be an explosive mix. By 1850, Belfast was already a
sharply segregated city with processions sparking sectarian rioting
periodically throughout the rest of the century.

With regard to church extension and outreach to the poor, the
Methodists showed more flexibility and were more willing to
operate in less expensive and more homely buildings. They had a
strong practical side to their evangelical fervour, often providing help
with clothing, dispensing food and doing much home visitation.
Death was a regular visitor to many families and this offered a point
of contact at the most vulnerable moments. The Methodist 'adult
class structure' was quite effective as a means of integrating people
into the life of the church and giving them some solid foundations
in teaching and mutual support.

The other churches did respond eventually but more slowly.
Many poor people took advantage of the material benefits of this
outreach but church attendance does not seem to have been a major
priority. Disincentives to attending were – lack of 'a suit of clothes',
seating patterns, social distinctions and the cultural assumptions of
those leading worship. Such distinctions do not seem to have been so
strong in the Catholic culture and this may partly account for less
working class alienation there until more recently. In the Protestant
community the work of the Belfast City Mission led to the setting up
of a mission hall in many parishes, mostly attended by the poor, or
less respectable, thus establishing a pattern of social segregation that
is still visible today. Even here the numbers of men involved does not
seem to have been very high.

Social witness

The impact of the churches, however, cannot be measured purely in terms of church attendance. Against a background of Catholic nationalism, radical politics and industrialisation, aristocrats, employers, clergy and Church people imbued with evangelical seriousness attempted to propagate a scripture-based culture that upheld social and political stability. They were motivated by fear of an underclass of godless labourers, as well as the desire to promote spiritual regeneration and moral elevation. In addition to the evangelical focus, their weapons were temperance, education, sabbatharianism, charity and unrelenting moral campaigns. They attacked many of the traditional leisure activities such as drinking, dancing, theatre, cock-fighting and boxing. They delivered tracts and bibles and they ran Sunday schools.

The emphasis in these schools was on class harmony, good manners, sound morals and respectable appearance. As there was no universal education then, they taught people to read and write (especially bible verses), and they took them on excursions to the seaside. They provided warmth, shelter and material aid. People recognised the value of literacy, and the cheapness of this opportunity outweighed the paternalism inherent in it. However, apart from short periods of revival, there is little evidence that it led to significant regular church going. In spite of this flexibility and enterprise, there is reason to believe that the poor were often alienated by the condemnation of their leisure activities, which they saw as their only escape from drudgery and misery.

At one stage drunkenness was the main target, and temperance societies, both Catholic and Protestant, worked on the principle that self respect was gained by sobriety and was therefore of great moral and social significance. It was a time when tearooms, reading rooms, YMCA and Boys' Brigade were established. The pioneer Total Abstinence Association (founded 1898) and the Band of Hope were active in the Catholic and Protestant communities respectively. There was an emphasis on respectability; frugality, temperance and education were believed to lead to personal and social improvement. Prosperity was associated with Providence. Idleness was seen as the parent of crime and the forerunner of poverty.

Class interdependence and sectarianism

Such a paternalistic approach disavowed social radicalism, which was felt to be un-scriptural. Christian liberal and radical voices were not totally absent but most of those who protested were regarded as atheists, heretics and/or later communists. Class consciousness was undermined by the Orange Order. Clergy supported the interdependence of classes and united with voluntary societies and employers in traditions of charity. Indeed, the contribution of the churches to voluntary societies at this period was substantial. Thus, by a combination of deference, moral coercion and apathy, the lower classes were encouraged to accept their place in a predetermined social scale. The self-assertion of working class Orangemen did, at times, put the conservatives to the test; the Trade Union and Labour movement did succeed in uniting the poor on occasion, but the sectarian forces usually won out in the end.

Aggressive evangelicalism often caused rifts in Protestant families over the expression of belief. Anti-Catholicism was widespread amongst clergy and laity and was grounded in local social and political realities. The Anglo-Catholic movement in Britain and the rising power of the Catholic Church in Ireland after Catholic emancipation led to strong suspicion. A key factor in this was the famous 'Hillsborough Wedding' of 1834 when the Rev. Henry Cooke proclaimed the banns of marriage between Presbyterians and Anglicans to oppose popery, nationalism and liberalism. Open-air rallies warned of imminent dangers to the Protestant heritage.

The Roman Catholic Church in Belfast

During this period the Catholic Church did indeed develop a strong organisation in the wake of the dislocation of the penal days. Many churches were built; numbers of priests and religious orders increased; self-improvement societies, Catholic colleges, dispensaries, orphanages and the Mater Infirmorum Hospital (1884) were established. Lay groups like St Vincent de Paul (and after 1921, the Legion of Mary) were active, and there was aggressive Catholic Missionary activity emanating from places like Clonard Monastery. Nineteenth-century Catholicism reflected the *ultra montane* policies of leaders like Cardinal Cullen. And although this was in many ways very suspicious of nationalism, the two combined to create, in the eyes of many Protestants, a monster of which they were deeply fearful.

There were political tensions both within the Catholic Church and between the Church, Sinn Féin and the Nationalist Party, as different groups vied for leadership of that sector of the community. But church attendance and loyalty was high even amongst working-class Catholics. The sectarian tensions, however, and the strict enforcement of the *Ne Temere* decree on mixed marriages, prevented any significant integration. The bitter controversy surrounding the McCann mixed marriage case in Belfast polarised the two communities and confirmed protestant fears of 'Rome Rule'. At the time of partition, 8,000 Catholics were expelled from the Belfast shipyard on the grounds that they were disloyal to partition and the new government. Some Protestant socialists were also expelled because they were seen as not sufficiently loyal. The result was that many Catholic families were reduced to extreme poverty. (Police reports indicate that as many as 50,000 people were affected and many sought sanctuary in the new Irish Free State). Sectarian violence at this period led to many deaths. Catholics perceived it as an armed pogrom led by the notorious B-specials. Protestant leaders, on the other hand, saw it as a 'siege' by the IRA. The resulting bitterness has been long lasting and has coloured Catholic/Nationalist attitudes to the new State for decades. Poverty, however, was widespread amongst all working-class people during the depression of the thirties.

A state within a state

The combination of all these factors, political, social and sectarian, led to the Catholic community becoming a state within a state, with their own social infrastructure of church, schools, newspapers, Gaelic Athletic Association (GAA), Ancient Order of Hibernians (AOH), The Mater Hospital, Irish language, etc. However, in spite of their differences, it is noteworthy that both Protestant and Catholic traditions had some strong common features, i.e. a self-conscious reliance on female piety, a strong belief in the religious and social utility of education, a commitment to Holy Charity, and the pursuit of religious respectability. Although the numbers of Catholic churches were fewer, they were larger and more imposing, all of which tended to confirm the Protestant stereotype of authoritarianism. Their assiduous public collections to fund these new structures (more necessary because of the smaller numbers of Catholic businessmen) were seen by many Protestants as exploitation of the poor, and the dominance of Italianate forms of devotion were regarded as alien.

The reality was that the Catholic Church was far from the aggressive monolith that the Protestants perceived. They were deeply fearful of Protestant proselytism and were beset with many internal fears and divisions. The retention of Catholic schools was partly the result of this but it may also have contributed to a closer link between the Church and the working class in the long run. During this period conflicts were often kept alive by processions and festivals and this was the period when the tradition of 'control' became associated with where you could walk. Of course, similar tensions existed in Glasgow, Liverpool and New York until well into the twentieth century, but the political tensions that fed them remained unresolved in Belfast. The Home Rule and anti-Home Rule struggles of 1912–14, the rise of the UVF and the Irish volunteers, and the invective of politicians and churchmen on both sides all kept the pot boiling.

It is difficult to assess the influence of various revivals in nineteenth and early twentieth-century Belfast on the working class communities. Their emphasis was very much focused on individual salvation and on personal morality. They certainly did affect many people at the time but it is hard to judge how long lasting they were. At one point Harland and Wolf had to build a large shed to contain all the returned stolen goods that were handed in when guilty consciences were aroused! However, there does not seem to have been much emphasis on the fruits of the gospel as right relationships with neighbour and enemies.

Post partition and secularisation

The wartime experiences of World War I and II did lead to some mellowing of the conflict as a result of shared service in the British army, the shared suffering during the blitz and in the wider European struggle against fascism. This was short lived, however, and old antagonisms quickly reasserted themselves after 1945. The development of the welfare state offered new opportunity for all, but at the same time it widened the scope for misuse of powers and discrimination in housing, which eventually led to the civil rights movement. Vatican II and the O'Neill era of Unionism (post-1963) led to many new relationships across the divide and the Churches' Industrial Council was an example of cooperation across the board on unemployment. Unfortunately, conservative Protestants perceived the civil rights movement as a threat to the state and the Union, and this led to the recent conflict and the revival of the IRA. Tragically, once again the working classes were divided.

During the latter part of the twentieth century, working-class culture has become more secularised, though the ingrained sectarianism is sometimes more intense amongst the non-churchgoing than it is amongst those who have retained a church connection, with the possible exception of groups like the Free Presbyterians. There are, however, many other influences at work. As older worldviews break down, community life becomes more fragmented and family breakdown more widespread. Domestic violence is now being confronted with greater honesty, but the more insidious gods of materialism have eroded some of the good values of earlier years.

There is, unfortunately, a legacy of warped images of the church. Many people associate it with a series of 'thou shall nots' and with bans on drinking, gambling, dancing and general fun! They connect church with 'soul salvation', exclusiveness and a desire to avoid contamination by the world. Their actual experiences are often with the pietistic or with very middle-class respectability and affluence, which does not find expression in solidarity, support, acceptance, forgiveness and compassion. There are, however, some paradoxes here. Where churches and clergy have sought to break down sectarianism they have sometimes been accused of betraying their people and failing to support hard-line political views. The Catholic Church has had a similar problem when opposition to IRA violence has been taken to mean lack of solidarity with oppressed people!

All of this raises important questions about how one is to minister to communities that have formed their identities through a history of antagonism. There is a tension between the need to identify with the needs and grievances of each community and the need to lead all to a wider vision of reconciliation. The fragmentation of political traditions may well be a necessary stage in the journey towards a new society. (We can see some examples of this in the new Loyalist parties that have emerged recently.)

In the midst of all these changes, it is remarkable that respect for the person of Jesus, as distinct from the Church, remains relatively high. Also, people have a basic capacity to recognise authentic Christian witness when they meet it. All of the churches are facing real challenges here, but there are also opportunities for imaginative steps, if we are willing to face the realities with courage faith and humility. Amongst other things, it will mean discerning where the spirit is already at work ahead of us, and being willing to consider a wider definition of what it means to be 'Church' in the many and varied ways and in different situations.

Notes

1   Much of this article is based on their material and on Oliver Rafferty's
     Catholicism in Ulster 1603–1983. I am also indebted to Dr Eamon Phoenix
     of Stranmillis College history department for further suggestions.

PART THREE

FAITH RESPONSES
TO THE CULTURAL REALITY

Introduction

Donal McKeown

THE EXODUS experience was not just a key part of the folk memory, which the Jews retained and celebrated. It is also one of the great paradigms of human experience. It is a rich story with profound echoes in many individual and communal experiences. The people in slavery who are so demoralised that they do not want to escape, or to believe that there might be something better. The problems – at the Red Sea and in the desert – that have them harking back to the good old days in servitude. The quicksand of relative comfort can be the enemy of growth, hope and discovery.

While some in the churches have looked back longingly to the way things were, to the imagined Golden Age, others have sought to strike out with a mixture of trepidation and confidence in the power of the Gospel and the wisdom of the Spirit. They have tried to dialogue with the situation where people find themselves, listening rather than talking. They have made mistakes. They have, at times, wondered whether they were wasting their time. The desert experience is rarely a pleasant one – but it is the only one from slavery to the Promised Land.

This turmoil and searching within churches has not been unique to them. Much investigation has taken place in other areas of life, such as the behavioural sciences and management theory. The results of such research may well have implications for how churches can facilitate the creation of an appropriate environment within which faith can be handed on.

Two points are worth noting. Firstly, some work in the area of social anthropology has shown how the social environment in which we live can have major influence on how we perceive ideas. It is clear that the role of peer pressure – at whatever age – can affect ideas and behaviour. Feeling accepted and having identity within a social context is a powerful human desire. However, this influence also appears to work on a more sub-conscious level. In societies and groups with a strong sense of cohesion and identity, symbolic language and behaviour are perceived as meaningful. In loosely structured communities, these potent channels of communication do not play a major role. The implication is that *belonging* can be a major element that facilitates *believing*. Clearly, there can be many unhealthy uses of such sense of community – but the proclamation of the Word and the commemoration of Christ's saving actions remain a healthy prophetic force against the oppressive rather than liberating exploitation of such forces. The challenge in fragmented western society is to build communities where the shared language of the Scriptures can find rich soil.

Secondly, management theorists have attempted to understand what makes for a successful company that learns to cope with the rapidly changing conditions of the market. Much of the work done in this area in the last decade has proposed that the successful business is the one that taps into the key source of creativity in people – their spiritual energy! Much of the emphasis has now moved from the 'personality ethic' in successful business people (how to strike the right pose that will make people more pliable) to the 'character ethic', which values integrity, the search for truth and compassion. The rediscovery of the spiritual at the heart of the secular world suggests that there are more openings than one might have thought for those who would proclaim the life-giving Gospel.

This would all seem to suggest that the following:

- Modern society is not any more definitively pagan than any other generation;
- While many people yearn for a spirituality, however, many find it very hard to 'feel' spiritual in their hearts;
- The provision of appropriate social structures can create an environment where communion is experienced and religious discourse and commitment become possible and meaningful;
- Building open and welcoming 'communities of care' is a key way to helping modern people know God and salvation.

The teachings of Jesus of Nazareth seemed startling, even outrageous to many of those who heard his preaching and saw what he did. His brief public life, followed by his death and resurrection, shattered the mould in which the society of his time had been cast. It has to be surprising, when those who claim to be building a Kingdom that is not of this world, become excessively vexed if traditional structures come under threat. The call of the Gospel is surely to allow God's Spirit to be creative rather than conservative.

It is only at the end of the twentieth century that it has been perceived – at least implicitly – that the creation of *communitas* could provide the environment where faith can be celebrated and communicated. Consciously or unconsciously, various groups have moved towards the creation of such centres of belonging in the increasingly anonymous urban culture.

Congregations have had to go through long journeys to reassess their self-understanding and their mission. This has involved reflection on different models of the church as well as the changing cultural context. It has often included the adaptation of or complete restructuring of buildings so as to be user-friendlier and to enable partnerships with local community bodies to develop. In what follows there is no attempt to suggest that these responses are more worthy of consideration than others. They are not a comprehensive sample of initiatives. These have been included because the authors of this volume had firsthand knowledge of them.

The Changing Context of
Ministry in Northern Ireland

David J. Kerr

Grosvenor House: the new home of the Belfast Central Mission
THE METHODIST Church founded the Belfast Central Mission in 1889
as part of the Church's response to the needs of inner-city dwellers.
In 1894 it acquired its present site at Grosvenor Road/Glengall Street
and built the first Grosvenor Hall. A two-thousand-seat auditorium
still known as the Grosvenor Hall replaced this in 1927. The third
and current development on the site, now known as Grosvenor
House, was opened in September 1997. Behind these bold facts lies
a story of faith and innovation, unbroken for 110 years.

The second Grosvenor Hall was a well-known and popular venue
in Belfast for both religious and secular events, as well as being home
of the Grosvenor Hall congregation. In the early sixties it was still
possible to have capacity crowds for special services. There were,
however, clear signs of decline in the congregational membership.
With the onset of violence in the city from 1969, the congregation
dwindled away to a small core of fifty people. The large hall was
vacated and ancillary buildings were used for worship and other
activities. Being situated so close to the Grand Opera House and the
Europa Hotel, the building suffered bomb damage on thirty-four
separate occasions.

At the Mission Centenary in 1989 the congregation declared its
commitment to remaining on the site and to seeking a
redevelopment of its property. They published concept designs and
began a long process of exploration as to the best way to turn their

dreams into reality. Because of financial constraints it was felt that the best way to develop was in partnership with a developer. After many disappointments, however, the decision was made to undertake the redevelopment on their own.

The congregation made a parallel journey of exploration as it sought to understand the nature and shape of a faith community at the centre of a city in the closing years of the twentieth century. Links were established with a united Methodist and URC (United Reform Church) church in Stafford, which had just been rebuilt in the town centre. Visits were exchanged in both directions and people began to talk of the possibility of a new building. In the meantime the congregation continued to explore what it might mean to be church in today's world. A major step in this journey of understanding was a congregational conference held at normal worship time on two successive Sundays. Presentations were made reflecting our past history and reminiscences of 'the glory days' were shared by older members. The results of a congregation survey were presented in the nature of a congregational profile and there was a slide presentation of the changing face of Belfast. Time was also given to Bible studies on the nature of the church in the New Testament and the nature of mission as portrayed in the Book of Acts. By the end of the second Sunday a draft mission statement was prepared and read to the congregation in a closing act of worship.

On the first Sunday of January 1996 the congregation met to celebrate the Methodist Covenant Service. The service adjourned after the act of renewal of the covenant, and carrying the bread and wine, the congregation processed to May Presbyterian Hall where we concluded the service with a celebration of Holy Communion. It was to be our home for the next eighteen months. In July 1997 the congregation bade farewell to their friends in May Street and proceeded to take possession of their new building.

The building comprises a welcoming foyer with a restaurant, which is open to the public. A corridor leads to other facilities including the Chapel and the Advice Centre. There is also a multi-functional space that has the capacity for 250 people. It is designed to have a pleasing worship focus and can be closed off behind pine doors. There are three further floors to the building; the first provides rooms for congregational meetings, the second houses the Mission's administrative staff and the third is a conference and training centre.

Reflection on this process has provided a number of theological insights that have enriched the work and also developed the faith of the congregation. In such a scheme as this, the importance of helping the congregation to 'own' the new vision cannot be over stated. The development took place over an eight-year period with many disappointments and setbacks, and only a growing ownership of the vision between the minister, leaders and congregation was able to sustain it. This ownership now means that the congregation has varying degrees of insight into what is happening now and what can happen in the future and will also enable them to sustain the vision when the current leadership changes.

Another major insight was to discover how history could be used as a resource for moving into the future. The celebration of the centenary provided the opportunity for writing the history of the Mission and focusing people's attention on the events of the past. By using this in a creative way, we were able to see that at various points in that history, innovative steps of faith had been taken that enabled the Mission to adapt to changing circumstances and to grow. So successful was this ongoing process that people come to see that we in effect were not doing anything new but simply following the models of the past in seeking to relate in a relevant way to our contemporary situation.

In seeking to provide a design brief for the architect the parables of salt and leaven provided a challenging resource and insight. From them the simple brief given to the architect was for a building that in the first place is user-friendly, that is friendly to those who no longer frequented church buildings, and thirdly, flexible in usage so that all parts of the building could be multi-functional.

Lessons learned
In the first instance, attention must be drawn to the importance of blurring the edges between church and non-church. This is simply said but it leads us into a struggle between distinctiveness and engagement. It is a struggle that continues almost on a daily basis

when the question is asked, 'What do we do that is distinctively Christian?' Or put in another form, 'Does an over distinctive expression of our Christianity hinder our engagement with society at large?'

A second insight was the importance of openness. So much of being Church is done in special buildings and behind closed doors where we are protected from view that it was difficult to get the congregation to accept glazed doors and a broadly open plan approach to the building. At a very early stage it was discovered that openness also means vulnerability, and as this struggle continues, the congregation finds itself questioning the roots of its faith and the very authenticity of that faith.

Both of the foregoing insights lead inevitably to a concept of partnership and sharing where a congregation learns to see its buildings being used by others without the congregation exercising control over those other activities. Closely associated with this concept is the idea of letting go, and once again, this is something that Church people have not been particularly good at. Once again, the congregation is engaged in the struggle of learning to let go in order that they may see that the ultimate is in God's hands.

What has been described here is a process, a journey, and consequently it has no ending. It is a project to which the Grosvenor Hall congregation of the Belfast Central Mission has committed itself, seeking to be authentic Church in the twenty-first century.

A Conversation on the Way

John Murray

'For me the Way is a place to bring people to rediscover their Baptism. It is a way, one spirituality among others, a flower in the garden.'

BRENDAN BRADY has been in the Neo-catechumenal Way since it first came to the West Belfast parish of St Luke's about 15 years ago. He is recognised as the co-ordinator of the Way in the parish and general area, for several members of the Neo-catechumenal community reside outside the parish. Brendan himself is married with six children ranging in age from 2 to 22.

Since August 1998 I have been parish priest of St Luke's and so have come into closer contact with one of the newest movements in the Catholic Church. Brendan's comment about the Way as one spirituality among others comes from a remark of Bishop Philbin, former Bishop of Down and Connor (1962–82), who had said, at a priests' conference following the Pope's visit to Ireland in 1979, 'Let all the flowers in the garden grow'. It was a remark he had made in regard to the different groups that were appearing in the Church at that time. I had found it very encouraging and one I shared with the Neo-catechumenate in my first Mass with them after becoming parish priest.

Even in their short history the members of the Way have known opposition and rejection both in Ireland and abroad. Brendan spoke of the movement's exclusion from the diocese of Bristol in England where the local bishop spoke of their 'divisive' character. 'People say it's too Spanish or it's not our culture – it's too different, and so on. These are the objections that often we hear.'

Without going into detail, they have had difficulty too in the local area. 'Priests and Bishops too need conversion as to what the Way is about,' Brendan felt. As a priest in the diocese of Down and Connor I would have to include myself in that category of 'need for conversion'. Prior to 1998 I had said Mass for the Neo-catechumenate on several occasions. About two or three times a year I would be rung up at my address in our diocesan seminary where I was spiritual director and asked to offer Mass on the Saturday evening for one or other of the two local communities. Bearing in mind the words of Bishop Philbin I nearly always agreed. Having been very involved with the Charismatic Movement since ordination in 1976 I had known the misunderstanding that that movement engendered in some people. Consequently I had a soft spot for those who were in different movements within the Church or 'on the fringe'. It was important to 'let all the flowers in the garden grow.'

However it is better to look at the beginning of the Way before I consider my own particular perceptions and experience of it. The Neo-catechumenal Way began in the shantytowns of Madrid about thirty-three years ago. A young man, Kiko Arguello, who had been inspired by a talk given some years previously by Pope John XXIII, started it. Pope John had said that the renewal of the Church would come through the poor. Kiko had also come to know something of the spirituality of Charles de Foucauld, which had given him the formula of living silently in the midst of the poor, sharing their poverty and their lives without demanding anything.

So Kiko went to Palomeras, a slum area of the Spanish capital, and lived there completely alone for six months. After a time people started to ask who he was. Many of these people were poor. Some were thieves and prostitutes; others had committed murder and fraud. They noticed that Kiko had a Bible and a guitar and they asked him to read some of the Gospels. Kiko was amazed to see Jesus working very powerfully through these poor people, because before God's word they were not immunised, they had nothing to defend.

'That is often a problem in Ireland,' Brendan tells me. 'Here many people are immunised against the Gospel. They have heard it so often before and yet they haven't really heard it.' One is reminded of the 'joke' about the Devil not needing to convert people to atheism anymore. All he does is inoculate them with a small dose of Christianity, which prevents them catching the 'real thing'!

'In any case, from these early hearers of the Word Kiko formed the first community of the Way. Around the same time a young girl called Carmen Hernandez had come to hear of Kiko and together they began the first catechesis. That was over thirty years ago and today the Way numbers several hundred thousand members in virtually every country in the world with 13,700 communities in 8000 parishes and spread over 900 dioceses.'

'The Way arrived in Ireland in a roundabout manner. A couple called Claudio and Nenei Bandini heard the catechesis in their home parish in Venice. Claudio was a doctor and his wife was in the drapery business. They would have described themselves as very nominal Catholics but when they heard the Word their lives began to change. They left their jobs and in a response to a call from God to go to the nations to announce the Kerygma [Word] they were sent to Ireland. They arrived in Cork along with a young Maltese boy who formed part of the team.

'The beginnings were not easy. The couple did not speak English and the young Maltese lad provided translation. However, with his help they offered the first catechesis in a parish in Cork. Two elderly women were the first to respond. And so the Way was born in Ireland. Today Cork has several hundred members involved in the different communities. Killarney and Dublin also have communities. In 1986 the Bishop of Down and Connor, Cahal Daly, was approached in order to see if he would allow a catechesis. Canon Brendan Magee, the parish priest of St Luke's at the time, was approached and he agreed to allow the catechesis. Additional catecheses were given and communities formed in the cathedral parish of St Peter's and in the central Belfast parish of St Mary's. However, in time these communities merged to form one community, centred on the greater Twinbrook area and the parish of St Luke.'

I asked Brendan to explain the growth of the Way in those early days in Spain.

'When the Word, the Kergyma, is announced it requires a response from those who hear it and this consequently creates a community (*koinonia*). Since the people in those shantytowns were truly poor and their sins were visible to everyone, they immediately welcomed the word of salvation and the Holy Spirit acted on them. In Ireland we are more difficult to reach. We need a longer time to become really aware of our poverty. As a result the growth of the Way has been slower in this country – slower but nonetheless sustained and steady.

'What the Way offers is a path for the far away to discover or rediscover Jesus Christ. That is fundamental and I think we have seen remarkable conversions and people returning to Christ and to the Church through the Way.'

At this point we were joined in our conversation by two men of about the same age as Brendan who had also come into the Way. Danny and Joe had different stories but both had found great support and direction in the Way.

'I was baptised and brought up a Catholic,' Danny shared, 'but about at the age of 15, I stopped going to Mass. The Troubles had just started and so for me being Catholic just meant being an enemy to Protestants or to the British. After my mother's death I completely rejected my faith and looked for meaning in other cults and religions. Nothing touched my life. My wife at this time still kept going to Mass and through the invitation of a sister in the parish of St Luke I started to attend the catechesis when it was offered. I went with a very sceptical mentality, but couldn't deny that I was touched by the Kergyma (the Good News of Jesus Christ). It was as if I was hearing it for the first time – I was amazed that the Gospel and the Church had the answers I had been seeking for some time. I began a journey with a group of people I didn't know and so started to see God working in my life and in the lives of other people too. That was almost twelve years ago.

'Another area that God touched me was in regard to having children. When we first entered the Way we had two children with the intention of not having anymore. Why bring up more children in this environment, was our thought. We couldn't even be sure our marriage would last. But over time God took away this fear of being open to life. Now we have nine children whom we see are not born for this life only but for eternal life beginning with their Baptism.'

Joe's story was very similar to Danny's in the early stages – born and raised in the Catholic faith, Joe too had drifted away from his roots as he entered into teenage years and young adulthood. 'During my teenage years I remember many Sundays leaving after Communion if my family were not there. By this time I had started to drink with my mates. Even after my marriage my drinking continued and indeed got worse. I stopped attending Mass altogether.

'After five years of this I knew I had to get help, as my drinking had become a real problem. Fortunately I did, but by then my faith was non-existent and I had become quite depressed and unhappy. I did start to go to Mass again and at the same time as Danny I heard the invitation to attend the catechesis to be given in the parish by the Italian catechists. I too went along very sceptical and full of doubt that these people had anything to offer me. Yet I saw something amazing. These Italians had poor English at that time but their preaching was truly from the Holy Spirit and moved me tremendously. The fact that they had left their jobs and families to proclaim the love of God in Ireland touched me. Their preaching was more profound than I had heard before and it gave me hope. They spoke of a loving God who did not judge me harshly and who wished to give me happiness.

'Because of the effect of the preaching I joined the Neo-catechumenal Way in December 1986 and am still a member of the first community in St Luke's, Twinbrook. Through the years I have experienced the love of God and His strength in my weakness, but also His patience with my faults. Sadly three years ago I lost the gift that God had given me and for a year I began to drink again. Thankfully I have regained my sobriety with the help of God and I praise and thank Him for this. I know all too well that my faith is still not adult and at times very weak, but belonging to the community and to the Church helps me to see God in my weakness and in the midst of life's problems.'

Brendan explained something about the nature of the catechesis that is mentioned so often in the writings about the Way as well as in testimonies by the members.

'The first catechesis is generally given by the itinerant catechists, in our case, Claudio and Nenei, and not forgetting Fr Pierino, fifteen years ago. As a result of their sharing the Kerygma, the Good News of the Gospel, at the time, our first community was formed. Most of those brothers and sisters still walk the Way with us, though some have chosen not to. That happens,' Brendan acknowledged.

'However, those who leave have been "salted", touched by the Word, and in some way their lives will never be the same. Indeed, some leave the Way and return at a later time to walk it more resolutely than before.

'After that initial announcement of the Gospel people are invited to attend the weekly Eucharist, which takes place in a different location to the parish Eucharist.'

In the parish of St Luke this Eucharist takes place in a mobile hut that serves other groups and activities in the parish. The two Eucharists on a Saturday evening are offered by the priests of the parish of St Luke and by Capuchin friars in a neighbouring parish. Other neighbouring clergy have also been faithful in helping out.

This raises the issue that often divides people and priests in particular in regard to the Neo-catechumenate – the whole idea of the separate Eucharist. Brendan explains:

'Members of the Neo-catechumenate are not encouraged to cut themselves off from the parish. Indeed, most are still very involved in their local parishes as readers or Eucharistic ministers. But the community that is called into existence through that announcement of the Kergyma has a special relationship, a bonding. At the weekly Mass there is a period of sharing called the "echo" when members share very honestly and deeply what God is doing in their own lives. It is a level of sharing which the big Sunday Mass could not accommodate. Our Masses often last for anything between one and a half and two hours – a bit longer than the parish Eucharist!'

'Gradually through this weekly Eucharist the person comes to understand their own weakness. He or she begins to discover their Baptism, to get in touch with their "old man" and to leave the corpse in the tomb and to be raised with Christ. But this stage can take several years. Indeed walking the Way is similar to the novitiate of the early Church with its various scrutinies and catechumenate stages. It is a process that the Way and the person takes very seriously.'

In December 1999 I had received a very generous invitation from the Neo-catechumenal Way to accompany them to the Holy Land in March 2000 where among other events they would celebrate Mass with the Holy Father. Over 90 young Irish members of the Way accompanied by several adults and priests flew to Tel Aviv via London. We visited the usual places of note – the Church of the Holy Sepulchre, the place of Jesus' birth, Lake Galilee, Mount Carmel. We celebrated the Eucharist on several occasions during those days – none lasted less than two hours, each was carried out with enthusiasm and fervour. The highlight for all of us, however, was the Eucharist with Pope John Paul on the shores of Lake Galilee at the supposed site of the Sermon on the Mount. Despite his obvious frailty the Pontiff gave one of the most inspiring sermons on the Beatitudes that I have ever heard. He greeted all the young people present but in particular the over 50,000 members of the Way who had come from all over the world.

When the Eucharist was over and the Pope had departed for another destination of his hectic schedule in Israel, the members of the Way remained on to eat lunch and then spend time with their founders, Kiko and Carmen. These two led the assembled youth in song and reflection for about four hours. Dusk was settling over the Galilee sky and the rain that had threatened all day began to appear. The Irish members of the Way had told me that generally at the end of these gatherings Kiko would make an appeal for young men and women to offer themselves to the Lord. However, as the rain increased and the darkness thickened I thought he would postpone it this time. To my surprise Kiko issued the call and for the next forty minutes three thousand young men and women approached the altar to offer themselves for the priesthood and the religious life. It was an amazing sight – and especially for me, who am also vocation director in my own diocese!

'I think the reason the Way attracts and keeps the young,' Brendan explains, 'is that they experience the truth that the Church has to offer. Outside the community they experience death. Yet they are not cut off from the world. They know peer pressure and temptation; they know what the drug world offers and the world of alcohol. But they also have a great communion with each other. They enjoy each other's company.

'The sight in Israel of those waves of young people going forward to respond to Kiko's invitation was very edifying. Naturally many make a response at the time but do not follow up on it when they return home. However, the fact is that many do. There are twenty-four seminaries in the Way and these are under the local bishop – they are not seminarians for the Way, but for the local Church. The girls generally respond by entering the Carmelite way of life. Their numbers too are incredible.'

Even after thirty years it is probable that most priests and indeed people in Ireland would not have heard of the Neo-catechumenal Way. With those who have heard of it or who have come into contact with it one sometimes has a strange sort of conversation. They admire the faith and enthusiasm of the members, but do not understand the need for the separate Eucharist and sacramental celebrations. Invariably they end their remarks with 'Yet the Pope seems to like it'.

Therein perhaps lies the key for all of us who will come into increasing contact with this growing movement within the Church. John Paul has spoken frequently to and about the Way in his many meetings with its members over the years. It is obvious in his sermons and in the time he devotes to the Way that he has a great regard for it. He recognises its prophetic call to the whole Church.

It was apparent from the numbers of youth from Spain, Italy and France visible on the shores of Lake Galilee in March 2000 that the Way is strong and growing in those countries. There are parishes in Rome, Venice, Madrid and Barcelona that have several Neo-catechumenal communities. These communities have restored life to an otherwise moribund urban church.

Perhaps in Ireland we have not yet reached that 'year zero' of unbelief and apathy that so characterises much of mainland Europe in regard to the Christian faith. But it is fast approaching. There are many urban parishes in Ireland – in Dublin, Cork, Limerick and

Belfast, where the practice rate has fallen below 10%. The stories we used to bring back from Europe about the declining faith are now coming home to roost. In Ireland it is a testing time. And yet we see many signs of the Spirit doing new things and raising up new initiatives. For the Christian it is always a time of hope.

Ultimately it is the Lord's Church and He is in charge, whatever happens. In the meantime I thank God for one particular flower He has allowed to grow in my garden.

Salt of the Earth
– The Quiet Witness

A: THE BRIDGE COMMUNITY
Helen Smith

Discussed and imagined in the mid-eighties, the Bridge Community Centre finally opened its doors at the corner of Ballarat Street in 1987. Situated in a predominantly Protestant area of East Belfast, it was an attempt by members of various Baptist churches to be a Christian presence in an area where churches seemed to be irrelevant. The trustees considered this venture to be an attempt at urban mission and wanted to serve the local community with no strings attached. Their intention was that the programme would evolve in response to need, rather than established in brochure form and shoved through letterboxes. Partnership with the community was something verbalised in recent history but present in practice from the very beginning.

Supported initially by churches and individuals, the project soon attracted government funding to coincide with dwindling support from disillusioned or confused churches. Eleven years of commitment to the people of the Lower Ravenhill Road has been fleshed out in programmes for parents and toddlers, young people, women, persons in receipt of benefit, those looking for work, the elderly and volunteers. The organisation has undergone many changes during its eleven years 'on the road', in name, location and personnel. It hopes it has effected change in the lives of people in the area. However, the people who have been changed most by this venture are those who envisioned it over a decade ago. In seeking the welfare of the local community they are finding their own salvation.

Planting a tree

There is a special tree growing near the River Lagan at Ormeau Embankment. A few women from the area, a religious sister, some workers from a nearby horticulture centre and a man from Portadown witnessed its planting. It is there in memory of a young woman whose body was dumped on waste ground at Ballarat Street Partying in the wrong house with the wrong people and being of the 'other' religion had cost her her life. As her Catholic father opened up the ground to receive the young tree, the loyalist women of the neighbourhood wept. They knew her killer.

The leader of the Bridge Community had sent a letter of sympathy to her family and to the family of a young Catholic workman who was singled out and shot as he worked in a builders' store further down the road. This family business never again opened its doors for business. On a night between his death and his burial a local flute band stopped outside his workplace and played an orange tune.

Mulled wine

Four years ago we decided to celebrate Christmas by doing something with local people rather than performing for them. We decided to go carol singing together. It's good to have shared memories.

Some people remembered Trevor's attempt to teach Alistair the finer points of guitar playing; others recalled the home-made lanterns carried by our American volunteers; Gloria voiced her appreciation of the liberal quantity of mulled wine that awaited our return, and others commented less kindly on our singing.

It was not a polished performance (a gross understatement) but the motley nature of the choristers made it both memorable and evangelistic.

Clean living and good living

Our whole reason for being on the Ravenhill Road was to attempt to give Christianity a better press so that faith and belonging to a Christian community could be defined in positives rather than negatives.

I asked some local women to identify the person who most reminded them of Jesus. One of the women named one of our workers and for a brief moment I thought we had achieved a measure of success. On reflection, however, I realised that while she acknowledged that for a period of about seven years she had been in contact and dialogue with someone who was for her an embodiment of the faith, it had made no obvious difference to her faith position. Another of the women volunteered the name of a Sunday school teacher of the 'good living' kind but in whom she could identify very positive qualities.

I had a lot to learn. I am indebted to the person for pointing out to me the difference between 'clean living' and 'good living' people. According to Kathy the former don't smoke, drink alcohol, swear or get into trouble with the police. 'Good living' people are as above plus they believe in God and go to church.

A birthday cake

I hated the bureaucracy of the ACE scheme, and was cynical of much of the department's policy, but am so thankful for the opportunity to work with some of the most interesting and disadvantaged people I have ever met. I was touched and saddened by the many stories I listened to of violence, abuse and insecurity. The overt and hidden violence done to many of the women on the scheme was beyond anything I had encountered before. The frustration was in seeing the pain and hearing the stories without being able to do anything about their situations. We tried to emphasise encouragement and celebrations – birthdays gave us an opportunity for the latter. Never will I forget gathering to celebrate the forty-something birthday of one of these battered women. When we brought the cake in and set it down in front of her I heard her say, 'Nobody ever gave me a birthday cake before'.

She was probably late for work some mornings, owed us money, and occasionally didn't turn up for work. If we had applied the letter of the law then we could have sacked her and many others, but what opportunities of affirmation we would have missed. As we took a gamble on generosity over and against wisdom or common sense, we may have been taken for a ride or considered a soft touch. But the Gospel involves taking risks in love.

I stopped managing the ACE scheme to take up the post of leader of the Christian Community. In theory this was to give me more time to spend with people in a pastoral role, but people rarely opened up to me the way they did when I was part of the ordinary things they did every day. Who says that God doesn't have a sense of humour?

* * *

B: THE 174 TRUST
Ken Groves

The church is situated in the north of Belfast City in an area sometimes referred to as the 'killing fields' of Ireland. This is an area deeply affected by exceptionally high levels of unemployment, poverty and sectarian violence. North Belfast over the past thirty years has seen dramatic changes, i.e. population shifts due to religious and social demographic changes. This has resulted in an area that now has more interfaces than any other community.

Duncairn Presbyterian church was established at the later part of the nineteenth century, along with many other churches, due to the growth of the Protestant population. As you drive through greater Belfast you will see many large gothic churches of this period that have closed down or have been redeveloped as commercial and private businesses. Duncairn Presbyterian was also facing a similar situation with the community around it now being totally Roman Catholic. The few members who travelled in (a practice common in many inner-city churches) found it impossible to maintain their traditional worshipping community. Most of their efforts were focused on raising money to repair this large building, a cost which became too much of a burden, and inevitable lead to its closure.

During this period the 174 Trust was established by a group of concerned Christians to evangelise North Belfast through its many programmes and projects. In 1982 they purchased 174/176 Antrim

Road. In the intervening years many projects were established that tried to address the needs of the local community. In 1995 the Trust took the bold step of purchasing the church buildings at 160 Antrim Road (formerly Duncairn Presbyterian church).

In the later part of 1998 the Trust began a process that was to have a major impact on the direction and ethos of the organisation. As it concentrated on its role in urban mission many issues were raised that the Trust continues to wrestle with today. The main change now central to the organisation's ethos and culture is the integration of a community development approach to all its activities. The Trust continues to be a Christian organisation whose value base remains the proclamation of the Kingdom of God through demonstrating its values in action. For the Trust this means working alongside local people, empowering them to meet their own needs and giving them the opportunity to make informed decisions. Central to this is the development of genuine relationships with individuals and forging positive partnerships with groups, organisations that together will have a greater impact in addressing the needs of the local community. The Trust states that this is the outworking of its urban ministry where it can openly demonstrate its values in action.

* * *

C: Developing a Community Outreach – Three Churches
Eddie McDowell

Springfield Road Methodist: partnership with the local community

The interface at the Springfield Road has long been a symbol of division and community conflict and represents quite graphically the deep community divisions of our city. It is here that Springfield Road Methodist is located.

The church for a number of years has been involved in community relations programmes. Since the appointment of Rev.

Gary Mason in 1992 a number of new developments have taken place.

Relationships have been forged with a number of groups, each of which is quite distinctive politically, theologically and culturally. Partnerships have developed out of these relationships and the concept of power sharing has been at the core of a new project for the development of the church building. The groups have committed themselves to an equal partnership in the management of the project.

In physical terms the scheme involves the church premises being cut in half; the entrance portion provides meeting rooms for the community and the remaining part is a refurbished sanctuary. The large hall at the back of the church will again be given over to the community, with its design particularly accommodating the needs of younger adults. It is hoped that this new centre will continue to develop and enhance the relationships and friendships that have been made in the last few years through its many programmes and activities.

A lot of painstaking work over the last four years has enabled this scheme to be brought to this current stage. Many of the members of this church once lived on what is now recognised as the Catholic side of the peace line and moved because of community conflict to the Woodvale area. With more work to do, the group believes they have the opportunity to develop a very positive model of Church, para-Church and secular community group working in cooperation in a cross-community context.

Willowfield Parish: a community development approach
The period February to May 1997 saw Willowfield Parish hold midweek community involvement sessions. This explored what was happening in their area and the needs of the community. They also covered issues such as: evangelism and social action, theological bases for community involvement, sectarianism and community conflict, the church and community development, youth culture and unemployment, and other relevant material.

Willowfield Parish is in East Belfast and has halls and an old tennis courts and pavilion located in a different site from the church building and rectory. Developing from the sessions above, church members and people from the community came together to look at ways of collectively putting together proposals on how the resources could be fully used to the betterment of both church and community. The proposals centre around job clubs and programmes for the unemployed, programmes for ex-prisoners, youth work, mother and toddlers programmes, crèche facilities, and developing existing resources so they can be used by other groups in the community, e.g. football club, youth groups, senior citizens, etc.

Ballysillan Presbyterian: developing youth outreach

Much of North Belfast has seen considerable movement of the Protestant population out of the city area to the suburbs, especially in the direction of Newtownabbey and Carrickfergus. Amongst the consequences of this drift has been the closure of many churches in the area, and more are likely to close within the foreseeable future. The church leadership of Ballysillan Presbyterian began a careful review of its ministry in the area in 1994 and concluded that it should put the development of its historically strong youth work at the top of its list of priorities. It was quite clear that the vast majority of the young people with whom the church worked had no meaningful contact with the church outside the youth activity, and certainly church membership was virtually unknown to them. It was also quite clear that the church was one of the main providers of quality community youth work in the district.

In due course this led to a clear recognition that, whilst youth activity and training were real strengths, 'relational' youth work was weak, and that there was very little opportunity for the church's youth leaders – or any one else – to simply sit down with young people and find out how they were (or were not) getting on. The attractions of paramilitary involvement were clear, and eventually in 1996 the church agreed to create a purpose built lounge within the existing church buildings, which could only be used for 'relationally-based' youth work.

Making Belfast Work (MBW) enthusiastically supported the proposal, and, after full economic appraisal, gave substantial grant aid. The local MP opened the new lounge in April 1997.

The congregation has accepted responsibility for developing the youth ministry on an agreed basis over the coming 3–5 years, and MBW imposed no unacceptable conditions on the grant aid.

'Conquer a new continent':
Working with Young People

Donal McKeown

A: A Cycle of Care

Brian McKee is Director of Youthcom – the Down and Connor Diocesan Youth Commission. He sees Youthcom at the beginning of an exciting journey as he seeks to build a faith development and faith support programme across the Diocese of Down and Connor. He is also aware, however, that a particular emphasis needs to be put on Belfast, where the bulk of the diocese's population resides.

Traditional youth work focused on providing recreational activities, giving young people social outlets and developing their skills. It was assumed that parish structures, schools and church attendance would provide the necessary faith development. However, rapid secularising trends have led to a situation where many young people sense little allegiance to parish structures. That is where Youthcom sees it role.

It all seems very laudable – and many clergy have been happy to hear that a diocesan body was taking on this task. 'But', says Brian, 'some of them thought that we were going to take on the task of faith development among the approximately 120,000 young in the diocese between 4 and 25!' Youthcom is very clear that this was not its job.

Brian is not just concerned with providing evangelisation to teenagers. His vision is for the creation of a structure of programmes that:
- build on each other;
- are parish-based; and

- lead to a building up of community and the Kingdom of God.

This is not to be seen as an indoctrination approach, but rather an opportunity for young people to walk together on a journey of faith and understanding.

Brian McKee sees the 'cycle of care' having the following structural components:

a) Ages 4–9:

Faith/sacramental development in the local Catholic primary school (which most pupils still attend); supplemented by participation in children's liturgies in the parish.

b) Ages 10–11:

The Faith Friends programme, associated with the celebration of the sacrament of Confirmation. This involves older children sharing aspects of their faith journey with the pupils who are preparing to leave primary school.

c) Ages 12–14:

The GIFT 1,2,3 programmes.

d) Ages 15–18:

Programmes such as Kairos and Education for Peace. These look at developing a sense of community belonging and citizenship, and taking responsibility for building a better society.

e) Ages 18+:

This age group will have varying needs. For some young people, programmes such as 'Search' may provide useful material, while others will need support in developing permanent relationships (through groups like Youth for Truth, or Care in Crisis).

The focus in all of these programmes is not just that 'Jesus loves me' but on challenging young people to see the implications of faith for social and community relationships. The emphasis is all directed towards building leadership and service, in the spirit of the Gospel.

That sounds like a grand scheme, but Brian McKee is aware that it means getting a lot of people on board. Youthcom workers cannot be parachuted in to do the job in 88 parishes! Brian sees his main job as being to develop a parish sense of responsibility for developing the programmes. All Youthcom can do is to provide support and training in local areas.

There is a clear awareness, however, that faith development programmes are not going to be a major attraction for many young people! In the urban context, the idea of the local parish may mean very little to most young people. That means trying to build up parental involvement in, and support for, these programmes. It means using schools as portals through which individuals and groups of friends can be introduced to challenging experiences. Brian remains convinced, however, that ministry has to be based on the development of relationships – and the local area (or call it the 'parish') is where most young people will have their 'mates'.

The problem, then, is 'how to captivate a captive audience'. Brian is convinced from his own considerable experience that the way of the Gospel is not to invite young people to something without inviting them to something afterwards.' There is a need to tap into young people's idealism and desire to contribute to building a better world. But while the young people of the 1960s and 1970s were protesters for social justice, that is no longer a widespread phenomenon among young people in Western countries. The key focus is now on building relationships and trust – community is the focus for communion. Brian is convinced that the Gospel provides sufficient challenge to motivate young people, tapping into their enthusiasm and energy combined with their desire to belong and to be acknowledged.

And if citizenship and challenge are key elements of a Gospel spirituality, then Brian is clear that a key feature has to be the work towards crossing many of the divides that mar the face of Northern Ireland. Cross-community work is not just an option; it is an essential part of any serious faith development.

That is not easy! It may initially involve single-identity work, perhaps with an element of community involvement. Central to this is the building up of self-awareness, and of confidence in the value of one's own tradition. This needs then to meet the challenge of explicit cross-community work, building up understanding and relationships. And where possible this can then be built upon by work on a common community or social project.

This is one way of putting into practice what Youthcom sees as the head-heart-hand format for learning. Faith can be built when people reflect, relate and act together.

B: SOLIDARITY ON THE JOURNEY

An experience of pilgrimage

People have always held certain places as special. They can range from an historical site that has modern significance, through a place where some famous person lived, to somewhere seen as a sacred place. Each year since 1984 a group of about 1,000 able-bodied and ill or disabled people have travelled to the shrine of Lourdes in France. Different people will have different views on the validity of such pilgrimages, but for a core of young clergy and lay people, the annual journey to the South of France as helpers has become an unexpected focal point for a deeper journey.

Ever since 1858, Lourdes has been a destination for many millions of pilgrims each year. Some focus their minds on the apparitions reported by the fourteen-year-old Bernadette Soubirous. For others, the focus of attention is much less clear. And for the 110 young people from the Diocese of Down and Connor who go each year, there can be a very wide range of motivations!

Since the first 'Youth team' in 1985, however, it has turned out to be an important faith development opportunity. Ostensibly, the young people travel out to Lourdes to assist the 150 or so sick who are brought with the diocesan group, staying in either hotels with friends or in the hospital-like *Accueil* where they are looked after by the medical team that accompanies them from Belfast. It is true that, without the youth, the large number of sick could not be catered for. They wheel them around the various sites of Lourdes, as well as helping to wash, feed and generally befriend the disabled and sick. But no one gives up ten days of their summer holidays just to look after sick people!

The pilgrimage leaders – and specifically the Youth Team leaders – try to give the young people in their charge a very specific experience and an opportunity to discover the very unpredictable grace of God. For the Spirit blows wherever it wills.

The first experience that is offered is one of solidarity, of belonging. Many more people apply for places in the Youth team than are accepted. Those who have been selected are chosen to build a blend of experience and new faces, of music and other talents, of students, workers and unemployed. They are expected to pay part of the cost of the trip themselves. Only those who *really* want to go are wanted!

They meet for a training day. Getting to know each other, hearing the dos and don'ts of working with the sick, learning to recognise their own limits. A helper who collapses with exhaustion is going to be a burden rather than a help! Then there is the three-day journey overland to Lourdes, building up relationships, taking time for prayer, and clarifying what is expected.

Once they get to Lourdes, they don their uniform of polo shirt and shorts. It is hard work pushing wheelchairs in the heat or in the rain. There is a clear daily timetable involving duty rotas and participation in the pilgrimage services and ceremonies – with each day finishing with night prayer.

It can be hard to find space for peace and quiet. Being busy can fill the day very quickly. But time and space are needed. The young helpers are exposed to many people – sick adults and children everywhere, people from all sorts of countries, a varied throng pushing and searching, singing and celebrating. It can be exhilarating and confusing. They are thrown together with those who were comparative strangers a few weeks before. But the solidarity in work and in play is heightened. The young hearts, full of enthusiasm, are offered an outlet for idealism, for faith sharing, for friendship.

But the leaders don't just want to offer 'a good time'. A pilgrimage provides countless opportunities, openings for talking about God, for sharing faith journeys, for breaking the scriptures, for recognising the broken body of Christ among them. Most of the Youth Team will have come from homes with a traditional commitment to Christianity. The leaders hope that the young people will discover a new sense of belonging, of being needed within the Church – an experience often missing in the traditional life of the urban parish. They hope that confidence can be gained and new friendships made, where they can talk about faith, about prayer and forgiveness.

Raymond McCullagh is a priest and a university chaplain. He is convinced of the value of such a pilgrimage in solidarity. 'In this day and age,' he reflects, 'giving up one's time and money to work with the sick in the sweltering heat in perhaps not the trendiest way of spending part of your summer holidays. However, the effects of such activity are wide-ranging and outlast even the most impressive suntan. Pushing wheelchairs around all day, coping with the humidity, and the humility of living with weakness are not the best for the body but they do work wonders for the soul!'

In fact, there is ample evidence that those who have experienced solidarity with the pilgrim people – both able-bodied and sick – can bring something of that back home with them. Certainly, the leaders encourage the Youth Team members to meet regularly for social and religious functions. Some have become involved in other church initiatives.

Gemma has been there on four occasions. Now a university student, she is clear about what it has meant to her. 'Through the experience I have made some of the best friends of my life, very different from those I met at school. We share the whole experience and have been through so much together that it comes to the point where there is nothing we can't talk about. We share the same faith and the same beliefs and know without having to ask. Although my school friends respect my strong faith, I feel that the topic of faith is not something that we find easy to talk about – whereas there is no question about that with my Lourdes friends.'

Eimear, too, found that the experience of pilgrimage opened new doors for her. Beforehand, the traditional religious practices were just part of a routine. 'But now they are very, very important and I do not know where I would be without them. My life would be incomplete somehow. I have come to cherish every moment I spend with God. Every minute spent with Him is a minute well spent.'

Patrick reflects: 'Pilgrimage means spending more time than usual with Christ, be it through prayer, fasting, service or friendship. It enables me to re-focus my life, and to rediscover what is important. It may involve a lack of food or sleep, but recharges me in a way that no amount of food or sleep or indeed a holiday could. It prepares me for the next part of the journey of life ahead.'

Solidarity in service seems to a powerful opportunity for some young people. Believing is easier in the context of belonging. Shared experience and shared vocabulary facilitate discipleship. The Lord keeps calling. The challenge is for Church people to discover some of the channels through which he continues to call together bands of disciples who will embrace the reality of sickness in the world, who will 'be with him and go out to preach.' (Mk 3:14)

PART FOUR

ECUMENICAL/CROSS-COMMUNITY RESPONSES

Introduction

John Morrow

BECAUSE OF the intense polarisation in socially disadvantaged areas of the city, most responses to the urban cultural frontier probably have to begin in specifically Protestant or Catholic areas. There have been quite a number of ecumenical developments between middle-class congregations that are not specifically relevant to this study. We did, however, come across some very significant cross-community initiatives in the inner urban area and some other examples of shared witness. A fairly full account of the Forthspring project, which straddles the peace line in West Belfast, is given below. We have also included a youth project that has brought together a number of young people and built some strong relationships, entitled Craic with Christ. A short article on the witness of the Clonard Monastery describes some important inner-city and cross-community work. In particular, a twinning project with Fitzroy Presbyterian Church has led to new awareness of each other's faith and culture and joint action on some important issues of justice and reconciliation.

It is worth mentioning some other movements and groups that have impacted in this area without including any of the detail. For example, reconciliation bodies like the Corrymeela Community have brought together family and youth groups from inner-city and outer housing estates, through residential stays at their centre in Ballycastle, and these have led to the development of local cross-community support groups at flash points between Nationalist and Loyalist districts. These groups, often known as 'over the wall gangs' have often defused tensions during the 'marching' season and shared prayer and friendship has been an important aspect of their common witness. Other groups working from a Christian base such as the Link Resource Centre (Shore Road) and the YMCA have been involved in cross-community projects with ex-prisoners and the unemployed. The Shalom Centre on the Cliftonville Road has worked for the spiritual and social support of the poor of all traditions. The Irish School of Ecumenics has initiated inter-denominational Adult Education groups in the North, South and West of the city. This is in no way a comprehensive picture, but it may give some indication of the wide diversity of significant initiatives from which some lessons may be learnt.

Walking the Walk in Urban Culture

Donal McKeown

Craic with Christ

The name 'Craic with Christ' has provoked a wide range of responses from people when they first hear it. To some people it suggested fun and hospitality, or perhaps addiction, or simply a contradiction in terms. It began with social worker/community worker/college lecturer Gerry Skelton when he was acting as facilitator in a cross-community project between St Agnes' parish in Andersonstown and Ballygilbert Presbyterian Church near Bangor.

Gerry came from a Catholic background and had taken the hard route to qualifying as a social worker! Involved with youth and community work since the early 80s, he had moved increasingly into the cross-community area. However, he was conscious that there were many community divisions to cross – cultural, social and religious. Gerry's approach has been more inclined to asking questions, rather than to propose answers, on the basis that it's better to be unhappy with the right questions than happy with the wrong answers. This has proved to be a useful route whether in a formal teaching context or in helping someone in difficulty to take responsibility for their past and their way forward.

On the way into the parish centre in Andersonstown one day, he passed a number of young people. They were of a similar age to young people in the hall – but those on the outside had no intention of coming in. Gerry's response to their banter was 'Come on in and stop moaning!' The invitation didn't work that time – but it set his mind thinking. Working with the 'insiders' wasn't easy, but the 'outsiders' had energy and ideas. Many of these felt 'disenfranchised' as regards church, but they had interesting stories to tell and Gerry believed that they could contribute a lot, if only they could believe that.

He talked about the idea to several of his friends. An idea began to take shape. The origins of the idea are described in some later literature as growing from how 'a few pained at the exaggeration of differences, the understating of similarities and the results of Protestant and Catholic division, namely death, injury and separation'. The result was that he wrote to about 70 people whom he knew and invited them to a weekend at Corrymeela in November 1991. In order not to be controversial, he picked 'Politics' as his initial theme! Gerry wanted to start with something 'real', and 'to put God to the test, if this was his work'.

The result of this first successful experiment has been an annual weekend on some topic that is connected with religious faith, but that is also tied in to the practicalities of living in a society divided in many ways. 'Christmas Cracker' and 'Revisiting our Routes' were intended to be provocative as well as intriguing titles! Anyone can apply to come on the weekend, but those who get to attend are selected from the applicants so as to produce a sufficiently wide and varied pool of experience. CWC says it is concerned with liberating the God we have defined, domesticated and ultimately restricted in our own religious terms, so that people can free themselves to get to know God in a more informed and meaningful light. That means people from widely different backgrounds being brought together.

When people come on a weekend, they come simply as themselves with their first name. They will get to know each other's background, allegiances and experience at some stage between Friday and Sunday. But they are invited to engage simply as people. The time together seeks to provide permission and time to allow those present to make sense of that which divides and unites in Northern Ireland. The hope is that they will be able to discover and create new ways of relating and being. The result can be the creation of meaningful opportunities to introduce, encourage and sustain real reconciliation.

All of this takes place in the context of a look at the God whom Gerry insists is so much greater than our 'gods' – and he aims to do this by looking at politics, sectarianism, and snobbery, in the context of a new look at the Bible. Jesus was a person who asked questions; especially of those who thought they had everything solved already. So that means looking for ways to get people thinking about the roots of the Troubles, rather than just at the symptoms, and then invite them to act accordingly. This implies focusing on the possibility of 'liberating responsibility' rather than just blaming other people or situations for things that allegedly cannot be changed. It means looking at the stereotyping of other people. That becomes a challenge when it turns out that someone you have spent time with turns out to be an ex-paramilitary, a member of the security forces, one of 'the other sort' or even a member of the clergy! And if the weekend can provide the chance to meet with fellow human beings from a different background, then there is the opportunity to meet again as people and to listen, dialogue, work together, becoming proactive in promoting a solution to the many divisions in Northern Ireland.

That all involves agreeing certain ground rules in advance. These include 'the acceptance of each person as having value, dignity, and being unique', and 'the right to make mistakes'. Each person there is invited 'to exercise mutual responsibility and accountability for actions, non-action and behaviour'.

That is all very fine, says Gerry, but taking people away for a weekend, giving them new experiences, and sending them off on their own, is an interesting but poor investment in real change. So CWC tries to model good practice – and to model a little of the love of God (or is it the God of love!) that it talks about. If people are to be supported – whatever their experience of people and of God – in their search for God, then the language and the prayer used should be accessible to people from various backgrounds.

That has taken shape in the outings that CWC offers at Christmas, Easter and during the summer. A group goes off for a day somewhere local. That may involve a walk, a picnic together, some games (which involve everybody) and some prayer in an informal context. Gerry says it is about caring, love and service in action, but at the same time challenging everyone there to take responsibility for themselves, their story and others. It is quite a challenge to do that without imposing or being domineering. People there are encouraged to show appropriate affection but to remain aware of the danger of abusing others. And because the aim is to be inclusive, adults are exhorted not to come without their children. The last thing that will help relationships is to focus someone's spirituality outside their primary domestic relationships and responsibilities!

But CWC says it does not want to be an organisation, even less a new church. It wants to complement churches, to liberate people to reflect on spirituality and theology. Its purpose is described as 'a momentum acting as a catalyst facilitating transformation of individuals, groups and situations'. And that means finding some form of 'leadership' that models good relationships. How do you try to model God as parent – and yet not exercise control or be over-protective? How do you provide a structure that works without succumbing to the temptation to build a personal empire that becomes self-serving, rather than liberating?

There is a committee of six members, representative of religion, age and gender, which prepares the various activities and keeps in touch with people. The committee sees itself not as serving an organisation but as helping people to liberate themselves and others in a search for spirituality. There is no 'membership' of CWC, for it is not a group or a club. Their aim is to be consistent in their treatment of people and not to force anything on anybody. People grow by being trusted, and by learning to both trust others, and be willing to make mistakes in the service of learning. And in order to underline the ideal of trusting people, Gerry himself has resigned from the committee, so that others – now led by Mary O'Brien – can come to believe in a God who believes in them!

People who come on the weekends or the outings are offered examples of how people *might* treat each other in the spirit of the Gospel. But no one owns God or has God packaged. Gerry is convinced that much theology is not so much based on the Gospel challenge to be prophetic, but simply psychological projection by those who propound it. For that reason, he believes that many have been turned off the Gospel, and end up hating 'religion'. We are all broken and hurting in different ways. But brokenness should not be a source of division between people. Gerry is convinced that people in Northern Ireland are all stained by sectarian attitudes – and that those who deny this are the only ones who cannot be helped. The way forward is for them to be helped to recognise where they are, who they are, where they have come from, and to believe that there are other liberating ways of relating to self, others and God in a more integrated way. This will be discovered by love in action and by accepting responsibility for oneself and for others.

Gerry recognises that CWC does not offer some panacea for Northern Ireland's problems. He acknowledges that he may be criticised for suggesting some 'lowest-common-denominator' approach to faith. He is also aware that CWC could be accused of modelling bad practice because it has few people from ethnic minority backgrounds. The title may seem as having 'Irish' resonances in the word 'craic' and be exclusive in the prominence given to the name of Christ. However, the title is intended to be provocative and intriguing, rather than definitive of any content.

This is one person's experiment in being true to his own convictions, seeking to be prophetic. Like the first weekend, Gerry believes that the whole CWC work will fail if it is not of God. He sees CWC in the context of other work, which is centred on Gerry's part-time Tredagh House Ministries. These all involve taking calculated risks to facilitate growth and unexpected relationships. It takes good judgement to strike the balance between allowing people to take responsibility, and leaving them to sink or swim. But Gerry Skelton has an intriguing personal journey behind him. He believes that he has a long way to go. And he dearly wants to invite other people to share some of their journeys with him and with each other.

The Forthspring Initiative

Shelagh Livingstone

SITTING ON THE PEACE-LINE on the Springfield Road in West Belfast is Forthspring, an exciting, challenging new venture in ecumenical reconciliation and cross-community outreach. Forthspring was born out of the coming together of the Springfield Methodist church, Cornerstone and Currach (both Christian, ecumenical communities) and MISCA a local community initiative.

The Springfield Methodist Church
In the 1950s this was a thriving congregation in inadequate premises. A new building was opened in the mid-fifties, seating 300 to 400 people. With the advent of violent conflict many families moved away. All shops on Springfield Road above what is now Lanark Way were destroyed and demolished, the dividing wall gradually became more solid as roads were closed off. By 1990 the church building itself formed part of the peace-line, with its front door opening on the Catholic/Nationalist side of the community and its back door on the Protestant/Unionist side. Because of security fencing, access was only through the front. There was much violence on the road and many people were killed. There was constant stone throwing, frequent security patrols and vandalism, including frequent attacks on the church. There was a lack of amenities in the area; no public space for people to meet if they wanted to, no play areas for children, no recreational facilities, and no shops. The regular worshipping congregation had dwindled to 30, of whom 10 were senior citizens and about 8 were children under the age of twelve. Most weeknight activities ceased.

Under the leadership of the minister (at that time Rev. Sidney Callaghan) they began to wrestle with some questions. What does God want us to do in this situation? Is it significant that we are the only church on the Springfield Road? How do we work out the command to love our neighbour? Can we contribute to 'fullness of life' for community? Should we (the practical and scary question) open our buildings for use by people on both sides of community?

An early, visionary floating of dreams proved counter-productive, when a drawing was made of a possibility that included locating a post office on church premises. Shock, horror. 'A house of prayer . . . you have made it a den of thieves!' The underlying reality was a legitimate fear. All the local post offices had suffered frequent violent attack, the nearest had closed. Back to the drawing board! In existing premises we started a non-threatening cross-community project – a senior citizens lunch club. This was an immediate success and is still going strong nine years later. This was a generation who knew each other before the troubles and wanted to be able to meet again.

Rev. Gary Mason (who had succeeded Sidney) posed another question: What sort of death will we choose? To dwindle away to extinction in five years, or to open our premises, redesigned for the purpose, to a range of cross-community projects and find new life in the death of the structures as we have known them, with all their dearly held memories? After two or three years of wrestling with these questions and some of their practical implications, the congregation took the courageous and resounding decision to choose life. It was decided to divide the church building in half and redesign the hall nearer the road with a range of rooms suitable for a range of activities. Later on in the planning stage the other three groups came in and Forthspring was born.

Opposition

Opposition came from a cultural base, but differently expressed. A few people left the church for reasons they saw as theological. The minister received anonymous threats over the phone. At least one Catholic member of the lunch club was told by two men outside the premises (not church members) not to come back or else. Attacks on

the buildings continued, ranging from broken windows to a major
fire – possibly just vandalism.

Second strand – Cornerstone

Cornerstone is a small ecumenical community committed to
praying and working for reconciliation primarily in West Belfast and
based in two houses on the road since 1982.

It is a house of welcome for many in neighbourhood and further
afield and a meeting place for small groups across varying divides.
The group had been facing together some of the theological,
cultural, social differences and growing together, often painfully.
Their early activities included monthly prayer meetings for people
from all over the city in premises provided by the Methodist Church
in the big hall at back, and cross-community work with young
people. Volunteers and members increasingly helped with the lunch
club, and later with a parent and toddler group that was set up
jointly by church and Currach.

One of their members was also a Methodist minister with some
preaching responsibilities in Springfield church. Another was a
member of the church. Consequently, Cornerstone had an input
into the thinking and planning and was supportive prayerfully and
practically.

Third stand – Currach

Currach is another small ecumenical community founded by
Noreen Christian, a Dominican sister (who is also a member of
Cornerstone). It is located crucially in houses owned by the
Methodist Church and bought when it was realised that if the
security gate on Workman Avenue were permanently closed, an
alternative entrance to the church would be necessary. Currach is
therefore literally at times the door into the church. In some cases,
Church members initially see Noreen, a Catholic, as a threat, but
increasingly as a friend. Currach and the church jointly set up a
parent and toddler club. Its premises are, at times, used for small
meetings of church-related groups. Currach members sometimes
worship in the Methodist Church. Women's groups in Currach draw
in church members, Cornerstone members, and a cross section of

women from the surrounding community. There is increasing interaction amongst the three groups at levels of worship, prayer, and sharing resources in terms of people, activities, and premises.

Fourth strand – Mid Springfield Community Association

This is a secular association dedicated to cross-community work with young people, parents and toddlers, and senior citizens. It was based originally in two houses on Springfield Road and had some interaction with Cornerstone, Currach and the Methodist church.

All four groups were looking for ways to carry work forward more efficiently, coming from a common concern to build a more peaceful, equitable society. All were aware of inadequate buildings, inadequate funding and strains on personal resources, but also the huge opportunities in the area. Through sharing concerns, ideas and expertise – informally at first – a decision was taken to go into a new venture together.

Each group would retain its identity and be equally represented on executive and management committees of the newly formed Forthspring. Funding was obtained for a building programme and some staff posts. The refurbished buildings re-opened in 1997. There are now a wide range of activities supported by local people and run by some paid staff, but also with the help of significant number of volunteers from both sides of the community.

Positives

There are some obvious benefits from this development. These include: bright new premises and an increased range of well-supported activities; a growing congregation, as new people see what the church is doing as relevant; constant learning from one another across many divides as we mingle in many situations, and the possibility and actuality of a more abundant life for some people on the road. We believe that it is a unique and imaginative venture in faith at a significant time in our history.

Difficulties

One cannot minimise the difficulties. These include: a sense of threat and fear of being 'taken over' by one of other groups within the coalition as they learn to share the use of one building; and the question as to where does authority and accountability lie. Other issues such as continuing attacks on buildings, contested parades in the area in the summer, and misunderstandings and differences of opinion amongst volunteers, can give rise to internal tensions.

Questions still to be wrestled with are: how open are we to everyone in the community? Does this include security force personnel, politicians of all parties, or do we play safe by making boundaries, and if so, where? Do we continue to accept kids who fight or steal equipment? And above all, what have we learnt on the way?

Forthspring would never have been born were it not for the slow groundwork over many years of meeting, praying, talking together, and trying out small initiatives. We learned to value the small at a time when money coming into Northern Ireland was putting pressure on us to come up with quick, headline-grabbing initiatives. We had to recognise the reality of the depths of mistrust between the communities and within individuals including ourselves. Language acceptable to one group is sometimes offensive to another; we all have limits to what we see as acceptable and need to help one another to overcome fear, dislike and rejection of others when these limits are breached. In a society traumatised by years of conflict, barriers are quickly erected in face of the unknown, so thorough discussion of new ventures is important before decisions are taken. We need to hold on to the vision when the going gets rough and to encourage one another by sharing it again at such times. That means affirmation, including under-girding everyone with prayer.

Traditional Catholic links – sacraments and schools – served the community well, but are no longer sufficient. The Church needs to be implanted anew into the lives of the people. Anti-Catholicism remains a strong feature of the self-identity of many Loyalists in a way that anti-Protestantism is not a defining characteristic of Catholic/Nationalist identity. We need to map the contours of Belfast urban culture, to see what are the doors and the barriers to religious belief, to seek to uncover the reasons why urban culture is increasingly resistant to aspects of the transmission of the faith.

Clonard

Donal McKeown

CLONARD MONASTERY, run by the Redemptorist Fathers, has, since 1897, been more of an institution than just a church. The church is not actually a parish church, but its outreach has taken many forms. Their popular and populist novenas and sodalities have drawn generations of worshippers to their church, which is near the corner of the Falls and Springfield Roads, and backs on to small streets that run in from the Shankill Road.

Shortly after the Second World War, a Redemptorist named Fr Gerry Reynolds set up an annual 'Mission to non-Catholics', seeking to explain Catholic beliefs to Protestants who came in a spirit of enquiry. That annual event continued until the sixties. Other forms of contacts continued – and since 1983 a group centred in Clonard has built up a strong relationship with Fitzroy Presbyterian Church in the University area of the city. Rev. Ken Newell is Minister at Fitzroy, and the Clonard group has been centred round another Fr Gerry Reynolds, a nephew of the earlier Rector of the same name.

There are about thirty members in the Catholic group, and they meet on alternate months in each other's church, often for a Sunday Service. It is a valuable opportunity to understand the theologies, practice and attitudes of the other tradition. That can all be very interesting. But for Gerry, it is much more than that.

Faith in a divided city, he believes, invites people to seek communion in friendship, walking together in trust into the unknown. It is easy to say that the Trinity – the love of the Father, the redemptive power of the Son and the Spirit of Love – is working in both traditions. But that does not prevent confusion and pain arising, and uncertainty as to how they might resolve a problem about the way forward. Gerry is convinced, however, that there is something very holy going on when Jesus is leading his Church into reconciliation. He believes in a God who delights in unity and diversity.

Difficult questions have arisen around areas like the Eucharist/Mass/Lord's Supper. It is not easy when God cuts the sectarian fibres from our hearts. Gerry acknowledges that there are major underlying differences in sacramental practice and theology between the traditions and that is compounded by a considerable lack of clarity, even within the Catholic group. He calls these areas 'the dynamite stuff', but it is precisely there, in the healthy tensions, that God can play his music.

Gerry acknowledges that the document *One Bread, One Body* – issued by the episcopal conferences in Britain, Scotland and Ireland – has been seen by some as unhelpful in inter-church relations. Gerry, however, points out that, while the document repeats the Catholic belief that the celebration of the Lord's Supper in other traditions is not a valid sacrament, the same paragraph 41 points out that the Trinity can still be working through those Church celebrations.

For the Catholic group, it has been a real journey of discovery. Gerry still sees them being at the beginning of the beginning – but he is very excited at what is happening. They are all feeling their way into communion despite their acknowledged differences. For the Catholics, he believes that the friendship in the Spirit has enabled their faith to become freer. And for the Presbyterians, he senses that the idea of Church has become more real, and not just bound up with the personality of the local Church leaders. He quotes Marc Boegner's principle: 'The Church must be Catholic or it will not be the Church at all; the believer must be Protestant or he/she will not be a believer at all'.

The 'single identity work', i.e. the Clonard group discussing their own issues, has had to face serious issues. He quotes, with approval, Marianne Elliott's comment that 'The Troubles shattered Catholic identity'. No longer could they see themselves merely as victims, but also as a source of aggression and violence. He asks why the

Churches failed to hold the civil rights struggle in the non-violent way of Jesus. And he is convinced that such questions have to be asked with a view to gaining wisdom, not to judge any one or any group – for God is the one who will judge.

The challenge is to seek a new identity that does not abandon people's cultural background, but which reveals itself as greater than cultural presuppositions and identity. Anything that is of Christ has to bear the mark of the cross. That is why the following of Jesus will always contain unwelcome and painful experiences. They have to be prepared to be counter-cultural for Jesus' sake.

One of the more recent developments has been the monthly appointment for the Clonard group with churches in the neighbouring Shankill community. On about ten Sundays in the year, a group gathers in Clonard and walks to one of nine churches that they have agreed to visit that day. The purpose of the 'pilgrimage' is twofold. Firstly, it gives the opportunity for Catholics to experience worship with the faith communities that are trying to live the Gospel there. Gerry believes that this has been a great learning experience. Secondly, it is intended as an act of solidarity with the congregations, which are often small, struggling to seek the Lord's way in a difficult area.

The Clonard 'pilgrimage' experience is a journey in faith made by people seeking to wait for the Lord's way forward in the desert of division and failure. A pilgrimage into a rich vein of life, seeking God's reconciling grace. Gerry sees that as life giving for those who are prepared to journey in faith – quietly, to small congregations, stumbling as they go. Gerry is also convinced that this experience of being a pilgrim people has been a rich source of revelation, of God's grace. In the wastelands of urban life, it has proved to be a spring of water for those who walk and wait in love.

Conclusion

Eoin G. Cassidy
John Morrow

THE PROJECT THAT has given rise to this publication arose out of a desire to facilitate those engaged in the work of church ministry and evangelisation to engage with the realities of the rapidly changing urban landscape that is inner-city urban Belfast. As was stated in the introduction, the study is animated by the conviction that all theology is contextual, that faith is always transmitted and received in a particular cultural context and that a faith that does not become culture is a faith that has not been fully received, not thoroughly thought through, and not fully lived out.

Strictly speaking, there can be no conclusions to this study. All that has been done is to record a sample of urban voices and urban faith stories and to document a number of faith responses. One can be touched by the faith stories that bear witness to the flourishing of a genuine spirituality, which belies talk of an urban spiritual desert. One can be saddened by the extent of alienation from Church affiliation and the lack of any sense of belonging to a faith community. Finally, one can be inspired by the extent to which the cross-community and ecumenical character of many of the faith responses give evidence of the extent to which, in a polarised society such as Belfast, Christians continue to seek ways of breaking down the sectarian barriers that hinder the effective proclamation of the Gospel.

The most valuable way in which to conclude this publication is to restate the questions that motivated this study, because it is our conviction that these questions need to be asked afresh in the context of each person's own particular ministry. Whether in adult religious education forums, the meetings of a parish council, or other exercises of collaborative ministry, these and other questions provide the indispensable context within which ministry can flourish. All theology is contextual and the challenge facing those in leadership positions in the Christian churches is to facilitate the inculturation of the Gospel that accords with the experience and language of each generation. Unless the Christian message is continually retuned to the wavelength of each culture it risks either not being heard or being misheard. Furthermore, people look to those in the Christian community to promote an ethos of discernment, one that is capable of distinguishing between those features of culture that have the potential to open doors to the divine presence in the world and those that can create barriers and thus need to be challenged and transformed by the Gospel. Each culture is composed of light and shadow. In a rapidly changing culture such as contemporary Belfast, the challenge of cultivating the virtue of discernment is one that has never been more pressing.

The following series of questions are listed as an aide to facilitating an attentiveness to the particular relationship between faith and culture in contemporary inner-city urban Belfast.

A. The Cultural Realities

1. Where cultures have been shaped by intense rivalry, as in very Loyalist or Republican districts, how can the Church reconcile the gospel imperatives of social and culture solidarity with the need to challenge sectarianism and paramilitaries?

2. Is the breakdown of the family or the wide publicity given to domestic violence simply a more honest expression of a reality that was suppressed in earlier periods?

3. Is the refusal of women to accept earlier behaviour patterns and roles a positive development that needs to be welcomed? Are men being helped to respond to this challenge?

4. Is poverty relative and is it particularly demoralising when surrounded by affluence?

5. How far has post-modern relativism penetrated inner urban culture in Belfast?

6. What are the resources to which people turn to sustain them in daily life? What gives life meaning and purpose?

7. Do church liturgies fail to connect with people's lives and the daily issues that they face?

8. Catholics often resent priestly control, whilst Protestants express a sense of irrelevance or neglect. What is this saying to us?

9. Why is there a feeling amongst many people, especially women, that they are not valued by the church?

10. Are Pentecostalists and other non-mainline traditions offering something important from which we need to learn? Or are they simply exploiting a vacuum in ways that may not be always spiritually wholesome?

11. Are local church communities being eroded by increasing mobility?

B.   Faith Responses

12. In what way are our church buildings non-user friendly in inner-city areas? Are they truly open to all?

13. Does our puritan sensitivity to any form of gambling or our fear of alcohol abuse sometimes prevent us from involvement in community partnership for the common good?

14. Does our theology provide us with a vision to work for the transformation of society as well as the care of souls?

15. Is evangelism best done by lay people who are sharing in the total life of the community rather than by the ordained ministers?

16. What can we learn from churches that have embarked on programmes to relate creatively to their local communities?
    (a) The necessary preparation with the congregation.
    (b) The listening and learning process to understand the social reality.
    (c) The difficulties that may have to be overcome.
    (d) The resources necessary to sustain a long-term commitment.

17. In spite of alienation and loss of contact with institutional Christianity, there is evidence of profound faith amongst people who have learned to share their vulnerability with each other and work for the good of their local communities. Are we humble enough to recognise and affirm this in new ways?

18. Are we still operating with models of church that do not fit with the changing social reality? Are we open to explore and recognise new forms of Church that transcend denominational and social divisions?

APPENDICES

Appendix 1

Statistical snapshots on the state of religion in Ireland taken from *Annual Report of the Irish Council of Churches,* March 2001, reproduced with kind permission of the Executive Secretary, Dr David Stephens.

1 Census Data Northern Ireland (non-Catholics)

	C of I	PCI	MCI	Other Denom.
1926	338,000	393,000	49,000	52,000
1961	344,800	413,000	72,000	71,000
1971	334,318	405,719	71,235	87,838
1991	279,280	336,891	59,517	122,448

2 Church of Ireland Population

1947	457,000
1965	403,500
1996	346,015

(Source: 'Report of the Commission on Episcopal Needs' in *Church of Ireland General Synod Report,* 1998)

3 Presbyterian Church – Persons of all Ages

1968	399,807
1975	379,000
1995	305,000
1999	284,704

(Source: Presbyterian Annual Reports)
Note: Most PCI statistics regarding persons hit their all time high in the mid-1960s.

4 Methodist Church – Total Community

1968	65,064
1984	61,099
1995	59,669
1999	55,839

(Source: Methodist Annual Reports)

5 Methodist Church – Adult Membership

1955	33,000
1960	32,000
1970	28,000
1980	24,000
1990	19,400
1999	17,000

(Source: Methodist Annual Reports)
Note: Methodist membership peaked in 1958.

6 Churches that have been growing significantly in the period 1980–2000 in Northern Ireland

	1980	2000
New Churches	100	3,800

(the LifeLink Network of Churches is classified under New Churches.)

	1980	2000
Pentecostal Churches	8,700	16,800
Free Presbyterian Church	9,700	14,700

(Source: Christian Research, *Church Trends: Northern Ireland and Scotland,* March 1998)

7 Growth by Transfers

Those churches that are growing are growing primarily by transfers from other denominations.

The analysis of the 1993 Belfast Churchgoers' Survey (F. Boal, M. C. Keane, D. N. Livingstone, *Them and Us?*, Institute of Irish

Studies, 1997) finds that only 17% of Church of Ireland attenders and 18% of Presbyterian attenders have ever been members of another denomination, but 67% of 'Pentecostal/Charismatics' (people belonging to the New Churches and Pentecostal Churches) and 68% of 'Other Presbyterians' (people belonging to the Free Presbyterian and Evangelical Presbyterian Churches) have come from other traditions.

8 Churches that have been growing in the period 1980–2000 in the Republic of Ireland

	1980	2000
New Churches	150	5000 in the Dublin area alone (estimate from one of the leaders of these churches)
Orthodox Churches	100	Several thousand and perhaps upwards of 10,000 (estimate of the Rev. Dr I. Craciun)

(Source: *Irish Christian Handbook*, 1992)

9 Young People and the Church

Baptisms – Presbyterian Church in Ireland
1959   7,115
1999   2,221

Sunday School numbers – Presbyterian Church in Ireland
1959   67,490
2000   34,291

Sunday School numbers – Church of Ireland Diocese of Connor
1966   14,858
1985   7,852

The 1991 Social Attitudes Survey found the following for church attendance for the 18–34 age group:

Protestants		Catholics	
once a week	26%	once a week	77%
never	22%	never	4%

A 1999 Church of Ireland Diocese of Down and Dromore survey confirmed the absence of the 18–30 age group from church.

The conclusions of a survey of 10 Presbyterian Churches in Belfast (*Reconnecting with a Missing Generation*, November 2000) speak of 'evidence of major decline in the number of those aged 25–44 involved in any core activity of the church between 1997 and 2000' (core activity is defined primarily as Sunday morning attendance) and 'the most significant decline has taken place in the 25–34 age group'.

Those claiming to have no religion tend to be of Protestant background, young and male.

There is some evidence among Southern Catholic young people and Northern Protestant young people that there are two trends: a tendency away from religion, and, among those who remain religious, a tendency to be conservative in matters of identity and belief (see *A Profile of Irish Religion* in Irish Council of Churches Annual Report, 1995, and the report and discussion of the conclusions of the 1998 International Social Survey in *Doctrine and Life*, December 2000).

10 Number of Vocations in Catholic Church in Ireland

1965	1375
1994	201
1998	92

(Source: Council for Research and Development, Maynooth)
Note: Vocations in the Catholic Church started to decline from 1961. The prospect is a long-term decline in personnel and hence an alteration in the relatively high rate of clergy and religious per head of population that has existed in Ireland since the 1850s.

11 Mass Attendance Republic of Ireland

		%
1974	Nic Ghiolla Phadraig Survey	91
1984	Breslin & Weafer Survey	87
1989/90	McGreil Survey	82
1990	European Values Survey	85
1992	AGB Adelaide Survey	78
1995	IMS Survey	64

1996	IT/MRBI Survey	66
1997	Catholic Church/IMS Survey	65
1998	RTÉ/MRBI Survey	60
1999	IMS Survey	57

When two or three times a month is the standard the decline is noticeably less than when weekly mass attendance is the standard:

Mass attendance – 3 times a month or more		%
1981	European Value Survey	82
1990	European Value Survey	81
1991	International Social Survey	76
1998	International Social Survey	73

The young are dropping most quickly from religious observance and there is an increasing difference between Mass attendance in rural and urban areas.

12 Mass Attendance Northern Ireland

Weekly or more Mass attendance

		%
1969	Rose Survey	95
1978	Moxon-Browne Survey	90
1986	Policy Studies Institute Survey	90
1989	British Social Attitudes Survey	86
1991	British Social Attitudes Survey	85
1998	Catholic Church/LTBS Survey	57
	(Two or three times a month	10)

A commentary on the 1998 survey in Northern Ireland and the 1997 Republic survey reached the tentative conclusion that there is a similar set of secularising influences affecting religious belief and practice throughout Ireland as a whole.

13 Protestant Church Attendance Northern Ireland

			%
1969	Rose Survey	once a week	45
		never	5

1978	Moxon-Browne Survey	once a week	39
		never	11
1986	Policy Studies Institute Survey	once a week	34
		never	15
1989	British Social Attitudes Survey	once a week	44
		never	15
1991	British Social Attitudes Survey	once a week	40
		never	16

A Belfast Telegraph Millennium Generation Survey of both Protestants and Catholics in Northern Ireland found the following for the 25-45 year old age group:

	%
Every/almost every week	33
Never	27

Note

There is clear evidence from England concerning church attendance that what people say they do and what they actually do differs. In England twice as many say they go to church as actually attend.

14 Statistics in Relation to Belfast

Presbyterian Church – Synod of Belfast

	Families	Persons
1963	50,222	147,431
1989	32,125	77,663
1999	26,277	55,096

Methodist Church – Belfast District

	Methodist Community
1963	34,106 (adjusted for change in boundary)
1988	18,690
1999	15,995

Church of Ireland Diocese of Connor – Statistics for Belfast, North of River Lagan

1969	70,977
1985	45,867

Decline in the population of the city of Belfast (Council area)

1971	417,000
1991	279,000

There is evidence (e.g. in the 1993 Churchgoers' Survey) that Belfast Protestant churchgoing is heavily characterised by 'commuting' (much more so than its Catholic counterpart).

There are suggestions (see Eoin G. Cassidy, 'Religion in the Inner City', *The Furrow*, February 2001) that mainstream Protestant churches are increasingly irrelevant to many inner city Belfast residents and some evidence that many of those who remain religious have shifted from mainstream Protestantism to Pentecostal churches.

15 Outside Belfast

The reduction in numbers in the Belfast City churches has not been matched to a comparable degree by rising numbers in the overspill areas outside Belfast. The Presbyterian Synod of Belfast lost 68,416 persons from 1963 to 1986 but the gains in Presbyteries around Belfast were only 20,853 in this period. The pattern is similar in the Church of Ireland Diocese of Connor and the Methodist Church. The movement of Protestant population out of Belfast has been associated with a large scale detachment from the church.

Analysis by Paul Doherty (in *Northern Ireland Politics*, eds Arthur Aughey and Duncan Morrow, Longman, 1996) of the 1991 Northern Ireland Census of those claiming no religion (3.7%) and those who refused to state a religious affiliation (7.3%) show that these are concentrated in the Greater Belfast area. Belfast and its eight neighbouring Local Government Districts all have more than 12% of their populations either claiming no affiliation; or not stating a religion. North Down has the highest level at 12.5%. Furthermore, within these Districts there is a substantial variation; in the Malone-Stranmillis area, parts of Jordanstown and Holywood, for example, over 20% fall into this category. The author suggests that all of this indicates a move away from religion.

It is in the provincial towns and rural areas (the West of Northern Ireland) where religion remains strongest (see, for instance, the

Report of the Presbyterian Strategy for Mission Committee, Annual Reports 1994).

Appendix 2

The Challenge of the City
An extract from the Report of the Working Party on the challenge of the
urban situation in Ireland today to the Irish Inter-Church Meeting and its
Department of Social Issues, March 1990, published jointly by the Inter-
Church Centre and the Council for Social Welfare, reprinted with kind
permission of the Executive Secretary, Dr David Stephens.

The Irish Churches in the Urban Situation

4.1   Northern Ireland

4.1.1.   The Industrialisation of Belfast
The rapid economic change of the early and mid-nineteenth century
led to the emergence of an industrial working class for the first time
in Ireland. The Churches never lost contact with this working class
to the same extent as did the Protestant Churches in Britain or the
Catholic Church in some European societies. That this is so is
probably related in part to the function of both Protestantism and
Catholicism in maintaining the social identities of the two
communities in Northern Ireland.

On the Protestant side the rapid social and economic change
seems to have led to the emergence and spread of a new variety of
popular religion, often characterised by a conservative theology and
by an emphasis on personal experience. Methodism had a clear
appeal to sections of the working class and Methodists were 4% of
the population of Belfast by 1861. There was a growth of smaller
Protestant denominations and a proliferation of Gospel Halls. The
Church of Ireland and the Presbyterian Church lost their near

monopoly of the religious life of Protestantism and this fragmentation has increased in the twentieth century. Competition for members and fragmentation went hand in hand.

In Belfast, Catholics were overwhelmingly concentrated at the bottom of the social scale, with only a small middle class. Presbyterians were overrepresented among skilled workers and the middle class, and Anglicans appear to have been evenly represented at all levels of society.

The increasing population of Belfast (87,000 in 1851; 175,000 in 1871; 369,000 in 1901) drove the Churches into a frenetic building programme, particularly from the mid-century onwards. The number of Presbyterian congregations rose from 27 in 1861 to 52 in 1911. In the Church of Ireland there was a big effort from 1860 onwards to build new Churches and establish new parishes. There was a fairly steady rise in the Anglican population of Belfast from under 25% in 1861 to about 30% in the 1950s. Similarly on the Catholic side, particularly from the time of Bishop Dorrian (1865), new Churches were built, and new parishes created. Large numbers of schools were also built. Religious Orders came to work in Belfast and were particularly important in charitable and educational work. In this period there was a significant building up of sacramental and devotional life.

The rapid industrialisation of the city led to a significant loss of contact with the Church among sections of the working class (it was estimated in 1886 that 40,000 in a population of 200,000 were unchurched). Already in 1827 the Town Mission (later called the City Mission) had been founded to reach the unchurched. Great stress was laid on the educational, physical and spiritual betterment of the poor. In the late-nineteenth century we have the founding of larger City Missions combining social concern with evangelical outreach, modelled on similar efforts in Britain.

All the Churches were active in the social welfare field, and in many cases were the only, or the most significant, providers. The same was also true in the educational field.

One area where the Protestant Churches were particularly strong was in youth work, especially uniformed organisations. The Churches Youth Welfare Council (involving the three main

Protestant Churches) was one of the pioneer providers of youth club provision in urban areas in the 1940s.

After 1945 there are indications that the Protestant Churches were happy to hand over much of their welfare function to the new welfare state. In any case, falling unemployment and rising prosperity did away with a lot of these needs; the relief schemes of the 1920s and 1930s happily became things of the past. The schools had begun to be transferred to the local Educational Authorities from 1930 onwards. The period 1945 to the late 1960s was one of relative tranquillity in the city; the Troubles had not yet broken out, massive redevelopment had not yet started to threaten the character of whole communities and there was rising prosperity. At the same time new estates were being built in the outer suburbs and efforts went into building new Churches in these areas. The Churches' social and leisure functions (provision of bowling and badminton clubs, etc.) became more important.

The coming of the welfare state affected the work of the Catholic Church too. However, the Church appears to have been more concerned with continuing its traditional welfare role. A number of reasons for this can be suggested: a suspicion of the State, a different social ethic, the fact that the Church was dealing with a poorer population, and a greater centrality in the life of the community.

Unpublished research carried out by Fred St Leger and Norman Gillespie of the University of Ulster at Coleraine in the late 1980s in the Protestant working class Ballymacarrett area of East Belfast has shown that the Churches are involved in the provision of a wide range of services, by no means all confined to members, including counselling alcoholics, groups for the elderly, a meals-on-wheels service, an advice service and repair work for the elderly. They also dealt with the Catholic working class area of Legoniel in North Belfast. In both areas the research showed that the Churches made a significant contribution to the life of the two communities and played a substantial role in social integration.

Other research by Duncan Morrow of the University of Ulster at Coleraine in 1989 in the (Protestant) Seymour Hill Estate and the (Catholic) Twinbrook Estate on the outskirts of South West Belfast shows that in both estates the Churches are a significant part of the life of the two communities (more so, perhaps, in Twinbrook). In a survey 73% of people in Seymour Hill claimed some attachment to the Churches, although actual Church attendance would be very much lower. The Churches are a key provider of facilities for social life in the two areas. The Catholic Church in Twinbrook is the major agency for social services, ACE schemes, youth work and community facilities outside the State. In Seymour Hill the Churches are the most organised groups on the estate and are involved in a large amount of social welfare and caring work and youth provision.

To the Churches' involvement in social provision must be added pastoral work by clergy and others. The Churches' involvement in the organised visitation of people at home and in hospital is by far the largest of any group in Irish society.

We can conclude that in urban areas the Churches continue to play a significant role in the life of the community in providing social integration, meaning and values and in the provision of welfare services and pastoral care.

4.1 .2. Religious Observation

Richard Rose found in 1968 that weekly Church attendance in Northern Ireland as a whole was:

95% for Roman Catholics

46% for Protestants

Eddie Moxon-Browne found in 1978 that this had gone down to:

90% for Roman Catholics

39% for Protestants

but in Belfast it was:

82% for Roman Catholics

33% for Protestants

It is clear that in many Protestant working class areas it was very much lower than this 30–40% figure. Frank Wright in the early 1970s asked several Protestant ministers in the Shankill area for their estimates of Church-going in the area and this ranged between 25% and 10% with the average being 15%. He also commented that it was striking how many non-Church going parents sent their children off to Sunday School and to Mission Halls – he might also have added Church Youth organisations. David Bleakley, in a survey carried out in the 1960s, found that attendance at either Sunday School, Bible Class or Church was in the 60–70% range among young people still attending school in urban areas. He also found that links with the Church begin to weaken sharply once young people commenced work. Wright also comments that the Orange Order was a much more central part of life in areas like the Shankill and Sandy Row than the Churches. 'It is not merely a political institution but a community institution with social and religious significance'. Paul Arthurs gives figures for the Sandy Row area that support this: only 20% belonged to Church organisations while 33% were members of the Orange Order.

Two quotations from Gillespie, Garner and Lovett's study of working-class young people on the Shankill may be useful in understanding the role of religion in working class Protestant areas.

> There is usually an identification with a particular Church or denomination and this would depend upon where one had been baptised and/or parental affiliation even if the person involved did not attend Church or practise Christianity.

> Although religion is unimportant in the theological sense to most working-class young people on the Shankill, it is important as a means of ethnic identification.

It would appear that Church attendance may have declined further since the 1970s. In the Shankill area it was recently put at 5% and the Reports of the (Presbyterian) Shankill Road Mission state that at least 90% of the people have no real contact with any Church. A Methodist minister on the Newtownards Road in East Belfast speaks of lower than 10% regular Church attendance.

Some figures from the Episcopal Visitation of the (Church of Ireland) Diocese of Connor for 1985 are illuminating. These deal with Belfast north of the River Lagan. In the Belfast area 15.83% of people in 1985 with some connection with the Church of Ireland attended Church regularly (this was an increase from 11% in 1982).

However, attendance in Whiterock in West Belfast was 4%, in Glencairn 5.5%, in Sandy Row 8% and for three Churches in the

Shankill/Crumlin Road areas 13%, 12.5% and 13%; Rathcoole was 14%. The Rector of Whiterock estimates that of his 'book' membership, 60–65% did not even have a tenuous connection with the Church. The Rector of Glencairn estimates that only some 20% of families would have any meaningful association.

In Catholic areas there appears to have been a general decline in religious observance, particularly in West Belfast. John Darby quotes a priest in two estates in the Upper Springfield Road in West Belfast in 1983, calculating that out of the 580 families who were nominally Catholic, weekly Mass attendance had fallen below 33%. 'Non-attendance had lost its stigma, indeed there was social pressure, especially on men, not to attend'. In the Lenadoon area of West Belfast he quotes a claim by local clergymen that attendance at Sunday Mass was around 65%. 'It was also considered a considerable overestimate by some residents'. Gillespie, Garner and Lovett report a statement that the rate of those practising their religion in the Upper Springfield area is in the region of 20% and that the rate of young people in their late teens and twenties is significantly lower than this again. The Parish Priest in a parish in the Middle Falls estimates Mass attendance at under 50%. In the Lower Falls it is estimated to be in the region of 50–60%, but only 10% among young people.

Norman Gillespie and Fred St Leger's research in Legioniel, Ballymacarrett and Tullycarnet (a relatively new Protestant estate on the outskirts of East Belfast) found that contact with clergy in the month prior to the research (contact meant at Church services or in a person's home) was as follows:

	Ballymacarrett	Legoniel	Tullycarnet
Male	15%	21 %	10%
Female	26%	25%	15%

Membership of Church-related organisations overall in the three areas was 20% female and 13% male.

The influence of the Churches cannot be measured only by Church or Mass attendance or contact with clergy or involvement in

Church-related organisations. Duncan Morrow finds that the Churches remain important as standing for particular values even for people who do not attend Church.

4.1.3.   Numbers

Since 1970 there has been massive outflow of population from Belfast, some 100,000 in 10 years (30% of the population). This outflow of population has particularly hit the Protestant Churches. This can be seen by the following statistics (it may also be that the outflow of population is concealing a secularisation process – of people lapsing from religious commitment altogether).

Presbyterian Church: Statistics for the three Belfast Presbyteries show –

Year 1963	Congregations	Families	Persons
North:	26	18,298	54,371
South:	25	14,144	38,965
East:	25	17,780	54,095
Total		50,222	147,431
Year 1989			
North:	26	12,340	29,454
South:	20	6,950	15,091
East:	28	13,835	33,118
Total		32,125	77,663

These figures confirm that throughout the period there has been a decline in the number of Presbyterian families as follows:

North – 5,958 (representing a decrease of one-third)
South – 8,194 (representing a decrease of one-half)
East – 3,945 (representing a decrease of one-fifth)
This decline has been most marked in the inner-city area.

It is now reckoned that only about one-fifth of the population of Belfast is Presbyterian (as compared to just over one-third in 1901). The number of children in Sunday Schools in the Belfast Presbyteries has fallen in twelve years from 12,275 in 1975 to 6,158 in 1989.

Methodist Church: The annual statistics produced by the Methodist Church shows that the number of members, junior members, senior adherents and junior adherents in the Belfast District has declined from 25,951 at the end of 1973 to 18,690 at the end of 1988. The number of junior members and adherents has halved in that time.

Church of Ireland: According to the 1985 Episcopal Visitation Report of the Diocese of Connor, the Church of Ireland population in the three rural deaneries, Mid-Belfast, North Belfast (which includes part of Newtownabbey) and South Belfast, i.e. Belfast north of the River Lagan, had declined from 70,977 in 1969 to 45,867 in 1985. The fall in the numbers on Sunday School rolls was particularly acute, from 6,413 in 1969 to 4,192 in 1975, to 2,107 in 1985, a decline of almost 50% in a decade. The vast majority of parishioners are aged over 30. Indeed the percentage of those over 60 is 'alarmingly high', particularly in North and South Belfast. The number of clergy has also dropped in the Connor Diocese from 133 in 1969 to 100 in 1985.

Outside Belfast

The reduction in numbers in the Belfast City Churches has not been matched to a comparable degree by rising numbers in the overspill areas outside Belfast. The three Belfast Presbyteries together have fallen by 68,416 person from 1963 to 1986, but the gains in Presbyteries around Belfast are only 20,853. The pattern is similar in the Church of Ireland Diocese of Connor and the Methodist Church. Many people who move out of the city do not establish contact with a parish or congregation in a new area. This is a British pattern as well. Physical mobility is associated with the loss of active Church membership. Among major Churches in Britain only the Roman Catholic Church experiences little loss of active Church goers through moving house.

4.1.4. Inner-City Protestant Churches

The Protestant Churches in the inner city are struggling to hold on in the face of big falls in membership, with those that are left being predominantly elderly. Already a number of Churches have closed. A lot of Churches are kept going by those who have moved out of the area but return on Sunday to worship and are often still quite active in Church societies and youth groups. For instance, the Connor Episcopal Visitation Report shows that the percentage of families living outside the parish ranged from 8% in the case of Whiterock to over 60% in the case of a parish on the Shankill (other parishes in the Shankill/Crumlin Road areas were 27% and 20%) with Sandy Row being 45%. This development helps to create distance between the Church and the local community.

Churches are not only struggling to cope with the effect of a massive population exodus but also with the effect of redevelopment, the break-up of traditional communities, the effects of the Troubles and, particularly since the late 1970s, the effect of rapidly increasing unemployment (e.g. one-third of Protestants in west Belfast are now unemployed). The growth of one-parent families has been very significant: 30% of those baptised in one Church of Ireland parish in West Belfast in 1984–85 came from single-parent backgrounds.

The 1985 Episcopal Visitation Report of the Diocese of Connor said:

> The Parish System has broken down in the city. We must devise new structures to cope with the present and future needs. The Permanent Commission will have to consider new forms of ministry in the city if the clergy and the people are to have the encouragement and help that they need. It could well be that the Commission will have to think of a 'Mother Church' where there will be a Rector with Vicars or Curate Assistants to give pastoral care to a wider area than the present parish.

An attempt at restructuring Belfast parishes led to a mini-audit being carried out in these parishes. The Diocesan Council of Connor has now established a Belfast Priority Area Resources Group, a Belfast Priority Area Property Group, a Belfast Priority Area Training Advisory Group, a Mission and Evangelism Group and a Pastoral Council.

The 1987 Report of the City Area Committee of the Presbyterian Church said:

> A recent report of an Ad Hoc Committee of North/South Belfast Presbyteries points out that the three Belfast Presbyteries are so busy with their own organisations and problems that none has time to consider city-wide issues: and the extent of the decline of Presbyterianism within the city boundaries has been overlooked. Consequently no coordinated effort has been made to deal with the Church's mission to the whole city, and no Church-wide support is given to any efforts in evangelism, mission, social concern or celebration of praise.
>
> This Committee would, therefore, point out that this must become a matter of concern not just for local congregations or Presbyteries – but a concern that will need to be shared by the whole Church. Belfast must come to be recognised as a **Mission Priority Area**.
>
> As the Ad Hoc Committee's Report says, 'Large districts of Belfast are specially disadvantaged. There has been economic decline, physical decay, cultural deprivation and social disintegration'. In order to make the future mission of the Church more effective, Belfast will require resources beyond the means of its congregations. Team ministries with the employment of social workers, youth workers and other specialists may be found to be necessary. So, too, will the rationalisation of buildings and manpower.

Various Committees at a number of different levels of the Presbyterian Church have been engaged in assessing the growing problems and opportunities of the inner city and trying to evolve a strategy for mission for those who live and work there.

4.1.5.   Protestant Church Response

The early part of the Troubles stimulated a response by the Protestant Churches in terms of increased youth provision, particularly outside the uniformed organisations area. The Gillespie,

Garner and Lovett study documents this on the Shankill. Particularly since the early 1980s many Churches have had significant involvement with the Action for Community Employment (ACE) Scheme – several (including some of the smaller Protestant groups like the Elim Church) have become large employers. Some Churches have employed family workers. Others have set up drop-in centres, often employing ACE workers. Work among the elderly has increased. There have been some (limited) movements into community work and partnership with other agencies, e.g. Rathcoole Community Group was set up in 1983 by two local clergy who were concerned about the spiralling decline of the estate and the general feeling of malaise among the residents. There has been an involvement in permanent employment schemes, e.g. the local Anglican rector had a significant involvement in the setting up of a community supermarket and post office in Glencairn. The Presbyterian Church has established 'Friendship Houses' in the North, South and East of the City and has also set up the Clifton Street Centre in North Belfast to pioneer new forms of ministry to unemployed and disadvantaged people.

4.1.6.   Roman Catholic Church

Belfast was 26% Catholic in 1969, with 81% of these in the Falls and Ardoyne. The rest of the city was largely comprised of predominantly Protestant communities with Catholic minorities. In the enforced population movements of the early 1970s the general pattern of movement for Catholics was into West Belfast. The Catholic population became more concentrated in West and parts of North Belfast. In the general movement of population out of the city in the 1970s there was much less of a Catholic outflow. The population of Protestant West Belfast fell by 34% between 1971 and 1981; the Catholic figure was 16.6%. The Catholic population tends to be younger: half of the Catholic population in West and North Belfast is 24 or under, as against 38.4% of the Protestant population. One Catholic in five is over 60 compared with two Protestants in every five. Even so, Catholic schools are having to be closed or amalgamated.

Working-class Belfast was a remarkably stable world from the 1880s to the 1960s and this was reflected in religion and religious practice. The Church was a key part of the network which maintained social order and stability. This world began to change and to some extent fragment from the late 1960s and this has had its effect in the changing patterns of Church attendance that have been particularly evident in the 1980s. Large-scale redevelopment, the effects of violence and the rise of Sein Féin (particularly in the 1980s), massive unemployment (just under one-half of Catholics in West Belfast are unemployed), changes in traditional community and family patterns (for example, the increasing number of single parents) create enormous problems and disintegrate the community. The moral authority of the Church has weakened, particularly among the young.

The conflict between the Church and various Republican movements is a very significant reality in many parts of West and North Belfast. Historically, the Church substantially provided the 'umbrella' under which social relations were made in Catholic areas in Northern Ireland. It was the moral centre of the community. Increasingly in parts of Belfast it has found itself driven to adopt a stance as a 'party' in local areas. In the past it was above 'party'. Today this universal position is being lost. The Church has taken a stand against the sources of violence that threaten the community. As it seeks to prevent community disintegration and disorder it has increased its involvement in welfare, community and employment projects. The consequence is that estates become divided between 'Church' and 'anti-Church'. Although the boundaries between groups are not absolute in that the Church ministers religiously to many of the 'anti-Church' people, nevertheless the outlines of the different groups are very visible in many part of North and West Belfast.

What has been the Church's response? Particularly in the 1970s there was a big increase in Church youth provision. Groups of nuns came to live and work in estates, moving away from traditional charitable activities to provision of mother and toddler groups, mothers' groups, education classes and social and community work. Since the late 1970s many parishes have been involved in job creation projects, particularly using ACE schemes; for instance, Cathedral Enterprises functions as a co-ordinating body for Church ACE Schemes in West Belfast. There has also been an involvement in promoting economic enterprise, particularly in the setting up of starter units for small businesses, e.g. the Flax Trust in the Ardoyne, the West Belfast Enterprise Board on Kennedy Way, Glenwood Enterprises in Poleglass and Townsend Enterprises on the Lower Falls. Government funding has been made available on a large scale for these projects.

There has also been involvement in the setting up of social groups, e.g. in Lenadoon a youth club, a senior citizens' committee, a communications group that produced a newspaper, and an environmental group were all set up by the parish. The parish was also a prime mover in establishing a community workshop and creating forty ACE jobs. Catholic Caring was set up to raise money for projects in inner-city parishes and also to encourage Catholics in business and professional life to give of their time and talents. There has also been increasing advocacy by the Church for more Government support for deprived areas.

4.2   Republic of Ireland

4.2.1.   The Roman Catholic Church

The Republic until the 1960s was largely a rural society. The Church looked with apprehension at advances of urbanisation and industrialisation and there was a certain lack of sympathy for the industrial worker. Nevertheless, as in Northern Ireland, the Church remained in close contact with the urban working class. Mass attendance was very high. The Church had major responsibilities in the area of education and its role in social welfare and hospital provision was very considerable. For instance, the Catholic Social Service Conference in Dublin set up in 1941 by Archbishop McQuaid to co-ordinate charitable work transformed the quality of social work in the city. The Conference also established a youth service and was responsible for the provision of youth facilities in many of the city's parishes (and throughout the Archdiocese.)

4.2.1.1.   Church Attendance

A 1974 survey gave the following figures for weekly Mass attendance:

94% in rural areas

85.5% in urban areas of 100,000 +

The MRBI Survey in 1987 reported the following figures:

90% in rural areas

58% in Dublin

There would, however, be areas within Dublin where weekly Mass attendance is very much lower. Peadar Kirby mentions reports from some priests in working-class Dublin parishes estimating that only 10% go to Mass every Sunday. The Council for Research and Development of the Catholic Church has found that the groups who are least likely to practise their religion are those who are relatively highly educated, males and urban residents. It would also appear as if unemployed persons are more likely to be alienated from their respective Churches than their employed counterparts. Nevertheless the Church continues to have a key role not only in pastoral care but in shaping meaning and values, creating social integration and in the provision of welfare services.

4.2.1.2. *Urbanisation and Church Response*

As outlined in Chapter One [Chapter One refers to the first chapter of *The Challenge of the City*], there has been a massive urbanisation of Southern society in the last twenty-five years. Large urban areas sprang into being with little regard for the social, recreational and employment needs of the people. Family ties were broken, livelihoods were threatened and the ordinary social services and support that had been taken for granted were now lacking. There were all the problems of building a sense of community in areas that were previously green fields.

These new urban areas have meant a massive creation of new parishes, building new churches and schools, etc. At the other end there has been the depopulation of old city parishes. Many Orders have been given the care of parishes and also many religious have gone to live and work in deprived areas. Some are involved in employment projects. Over recent years many Sisters have begun to work full time in parish work. Many are involved in community development projects, personal development courses for women, youth groups, community play groups, home and school links, unemployment action and care of the elderly. The involvement of religious is the key to the success of some community-based projects.

The rapid urbanisation and changes in society of the last twenty years have meant that the Church is increasingly involved in a new form of social and community building 'that helps people identify needs and respond to them.'

One aspect of this is the work of the Catholic Social Service Conference. With the growth of so many new suburbs around Dublin in the 1960s and 1970s, CSSC saw the need to help local communities to come together and develop local activities. Resource Centres were provided in six Dublin suburbs in the late 1970s. These were in areas of high unemployment and acute social needs. A wide variety of different groups use them and they are administered by local people.

In evaluating its community development work in the early 1980s the CSSC decided that a better use of resources for community development would be to concentrate them on a particular area of need. The Greater Blanchardstown area – on the outskirts of north Dublin with an estimated population of 55,000 and six newly developed parishes with 60% of households dependent on social welfare – was chosen for a new pilot project. In 1984 two Sisters were employed to assist in the development of these six areas with an emphasis on personal and community development rather than on providing buildings. An initial period of research showed unemployment and isolation to be two of the major issues affecting people's lives. In response to these needs personal development programmes were initiated in the areas. In a second stage follow-up courses were provided.

The CSSC has begun to invest resources in creating co-operatives in areas of acute social deprivation. It has set up Community Works to advise and develop community co-operatives. Over the last three years this organisation has worked with about 49 co-ops and pre-co-ops with a combined membership of almost 200 people in the Dublin area.

The CSSC is also involved in helping local people provide services, e.g. on welfare rights. It has, over the years, changed its focus, 'We have become convinced that it is no longer enough to offer programmes based on traditional concepts of service to the poor. Rather the focus should be the development at both personal and community levels, on education and on the creation of a more just and equal society. This perspective necessarily involves a conscious examination of the political agenda. At times it prods the agency to adopt a critical position towards Government action and to advocate alternative strategies.' In recent years, for example, the Conference has published pre-budget submissions.

Religious Orders give relatively substantial sums of money to help local communities confront their own problems. The emphasis is on a high level of participation, promotion of social justice and addressing causes. The Jesuit Solidarity Fund is funding a project, Community Action Network (CAN), which engages in action, education and research that supports the work of groups based in disadvantaged communities and groups involved in issues concerned with poverty and inequality. The Conference of Major Religious Superiors through its Justice Section has in the 1980s become a major commentator and critic of governments, particularly at budget time.

St Vincent de Paul is the best known and largest lay organisation involved in responding to the immediate needs of poor people. Through its parish-based conferences and over 10,000 volunteers, it pursues its traditional apostolate. It has recently been involved in the organisation of government funded home management courses for women in poor communities and has also been involved in creating employment, particularly in the Tallaght area of Dublin. The Society in recent years has adopted a more critical stance in relation to government social policy and has called for more comprehensive and co-ordinated social planning.

With the rapid urbanisation and other changes in society in the south an old world is passing away. This poses very significant challenges to the Church and, in particular, to the clergy. The challenges are particularly major in parishes in the inner city and those comprising new local authority housing estates, which face acute social problems arising from unemployment, poverty and the lack of facilities. In many such parishes there is often little active participation in parish life; there is a feeling of anonymity; communication is poor; and the sense of belonging to/identifying with the parish is not strong. Initiatives have been undertaken to promote the active involvement of people in the life of the parish; to develop a strong sense of community within it; to encourage the preparation of lay people to assume responsibility for areas of parish ministry; and to create new 'structures' to facilitate these developments.

Some parishes have attempted pastoral planning and the development of parish plans. The Parish Development and Renewal Programme of the Archdiocese of Dublin was established in 1986 in an attempt to revitalise parish structures. Full time co-ordinators have been appointed in each of the Auxiliary Bishops' areas. The development and renewal is still at an early stage. The main concern at this point is still with devising and implementing some form of consultation with lay people in the parishes. A number of parishes have facilitated the formation of basic communities.

4.2.2.   *The Protestant Churches*

The Protestant urban population in the Republic was mainly concentrated in the Dublin area and was largely middle class. As this population moved into the suburbs a large number of historic Anglican Churches in central city areas have become, or are becoming, redundant. One of these churches, St Paul's in North King Street, which closed in November 1987, is at present being converted into an Enterprise Centre. The Dublin Diocesan Employment Bureau has two drop-in centres, one in the Knox Hall, Monkstown, and the other in St Anne's Community Centre, Dawson Street. The aims of the centre are pastoral care of the unemployed, job creation, and job placement.

The Dublin Presbytery of the Presbyterian Church has been running a youth training course in horticulture for the last eight years for young people from inner-city centres and the Adelaide Road-Donore Congregation has recently set up an unemployed resource centre. The Presbyterian Church has just opened a centre to co-ordinate its social work in the Republic. The Methodist Church has had a City Mission working with the city's poor since the late nineteenth century and the Salvation Army also has a presence.

4.3   The Churches and Temporary Employment Schemes

Churches have a very significant involvement in temporary employment schemes (particularly in Northern Ireland). From the government side the attraction of using the Churches is that no other institutions have the degree of support, cultural importance, general acceptability, and the local and national networks. They are also regarded as 'safe' channels of government funds (and in the context of widespread paramilitarism in part of Northern Ireland this is a significant consideration).

ACE schemes (and their equivalent in the Republic) have certainly enabled Churches to expand into areas they have not previously touched or have only done so to a limited extent. They have given hope and restored dignity to a few people. Nevertheless, their transitory nature and relatively poor integration into communities means that they must not be confused with community led and integrated support schemes.

The strength of Churches has been traditionally the strong networks of community and the sense of belonging that they provide. With temporary employment schemes Churches become 'agencies' with 'employees' who have to be managed rather than 'communities' with 'members' who belong. These schemes may only involve a small number of the parish or congregation. They may only give the appearance of expanding the Church's work. They may even act as a disincentive to voluntary help – for the introduction of paid care may lead to a decrease in neighbourliness and may cause division and tension in the community.

There is a danger when Churches become the central means of bringing funds into a community. The Church is seen to have considerable power and influence. It can be regarded as an agency of government. The power rivalries at the local level can be concentrated against the Church. The Church (and particularly clergy) are blamed for everything. Division into camps in the local area – Church and anti-Church – can become a significant reality with a consequent risk of alienation from the Church. How Churches act in such situations – how money is channelled, to whom, the structures set up, the involvement of local people, the role of clergy – are matters of critical importance. The best run schemes seek to develop local self reliance, initiative and leadership; they promote the dignity of people and provide genuinely useful work.